Praise for *150 Secrets to a Happy Wife*

"Practical, humorous, and to the point, this is the best read [my wife and I] have had together in years."

—Doug Wead, author of the *New York Times* bestseller *The Raising of a President*

"Entertaining and insightful from the word go; every dad in America can relate to Joe Gumm."

—Mike Greenberg, ESPN

"Most men are idiots when it comes to their wives, their families, their kids, or just about anything. Joe Gumm is an exception to that rule. His book is a survival guide for men—a funny, fun, must-read for knuckle-draggers everywhere."

—John Gonzales, *Boston* magazine columnist

"Okay, if I was not already happily married, I'd be after Joe Gumm faster than you can blink. *150 Secrets to a Happy Wife* is geared toward the male population, but as a woman, I read it and kept repeating, 'Someone other than my husband finally gets it!!!'"

—Tracy Farnsworth, Roundtablereviews.com

"Joe Gumm has learned that all important lesson...when it comes to women, giving a little gets you A LOT more in return. Who knew taking the trash out counts as foreplay."

—Al Learner, Daybreak USA IRN/USA Radio Network

150 Secrets to a Happy Wife

150 *Secrets* to a Happy Wife

JOE GUMM

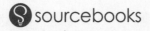

Published by Sourcebooks, Inc.
P.O. Box 4410, Naperville, Illinois 60567-4410
(630) 961-3900
Fax: (630) 961-2168
www.sourcebooks.com

Originally published in 2005 by Champion Press, Ltd., as *Romancing Mommy*.

Library of Congress Cataloging-in-Publication Data
Gumm, Joe.
  150 Secrets to a Happy Wife / by Joe Gumm.
    p. cm.
  1. Marriage. 2. Couples. 3. Husbands—Conduct of life. I. Title.
HQ734.G8847 2011
646.7'8—dc22

                              2010053371

        Printed and bound in the United States of America.
              VP 10 9 8 7 6 5 4 3 2 1

To the smartest, most creative, most loving and caring person in our household: my wife. I won't ever understand how you can have four unmedicated childbirths, with a baby as big as a basketball coming out of an area as big as a golf ball, and still be afraid of a roach crawling around on the kitchen floor, but that's okay. That's what makes you a great wife, mother, and friend. You're unique and special, and I love you dearly.

Contents

Acknowledgments

First of all, I would like to thank my Lord and Savior Jesus Christ for blessing me with a wonderful wife and four beautiful daughters. I give all the credit to God for helping me marry out of my league. I would also like to thank my in-laws, Jim and Jackie, for creating my wife and making her available to date and marry so we could have four beautiful daughters.

I am especially appreciative of the awesome people at Sourcebooks for their support, my human dynamo of an agent, Nancy Rosenfeld, and Brook Noel and Sara Pattow. Without these great people, *150 Secrets to a Happy Wife* would have never seen the light of day.

Thanks also to the people who provided ideas for me during the writing of this book.

Introduction

A burrito coming at my mouth at around fifty-five miles per hour doesn't taste nearly as good as just putting it into my mouth with my hands does.

I found this out years ago after I said something stupid to my wife and she launched a burrito at my head. I was able to ingest some of it because my mouth was wide open during the launch sequence, and no doubt about it, I had probably been spewing out more verbal stupidity while Operation Throw Burrito was taking shape. Of course my first thought was, "Man, she's got an arm." My second thought was, "If we're having pineapple for dessert, I better shut up."

About an hour later, as I was trying to figure out how to get guacamole and sour cream out of my hair, I realized I totally deserved a burrito to the face. I had obviously made my wife unhappy, and for that, I paid the price. It wasn't a fun feeling seeing my wife instantly turn into a baseball pitcher, but I will say it was the softest and warmest thing ever thrown at me in our fourteen years of marriage.

Now after that incident, I learned a very valuable lesson: *if my wife isn't happy, no one is happy*. And I also learned that bean residue is really hard to get out of the deepest, darkest part of your ears.

So the question now is, how did I make my wife happy after that incident, and how do all married men continue to do it until death do us part? A cruise? Diamonds? A deep-tissue massage from an expensive spa? How about a deep-tissue massage, with actual diamonds, while on a cruise? Well, if you ask most women what makes them happy, they usually say, "My kids." Others might say, "My family." It's rare, but some women say, "My husband." And then you have a very small majority that say, "It would totally make me happy to see my husband pregnant." The list is actually endless for women and way more complicated than a man's list.

We all know what makes men happy: *food*, *sex*, and *sports*. It's not an ancient Chinese secret uncovered in a Dan Brown novel, and it doesn't take much effort to fulfill the needs on this list. In fact, give us a pizza, put us in a room with anything sports related, and then after we're done with the pizza, give us two minutes in the bedroom, and the list is complete. Depending on the sporting event, the list could take anywhere from thirty minutes to eleven hours and five minutes to fulfill. I say eleven hours and five minutes because at the 2010 Wimbledon Championships, John Isner defeated Nicolas Mahut in the world's longest tennis match, which lasted eleven hours, five minutes. Granted, there are other things that make us happy, but for the most part *food*, *sex*, and *sports* are it. If you really, really, really want to make us happy, let us do all three at the same time.

Now for women, the list of what makes them happy is a lot longer. It changes on a weekly basis. Scratch that! The list may change on an hourly basis, and that's okay. If "constantly changing things" is something that makes them happy, it's on the list. The short-term goal here is to avoid food to the face at all costs (unless you can actually digest it successfully without injury). The long-term goal is to make Mommy happy 24/7/365. To be honest, the ultimate goal is to complete the man's list every day. But again, just in case you weren't paying attention, the only way we get to enjoy those three things on our list is to make sure Mommy's list is always fulfilled first.

Chapter One

Required Reading for Future Sons-in-Law

"She did everything Fred Astaire did, and she did it backwards and in high heels."

—Cartoonist Bob Thaves, referring to
Ginger Rogers and Fred Astaire

Every morning we play a fun game in our house called *Who Will Cry First?* It begins around 7:15 in the morning when our four daughters get out of bed. The winner is usually upset because she has to get *out of bed*, but the crying intensifies when she can't find her favorite sparkly shoes with the pretty pink bows.

It's the exact same thing at night. When I want to hear high-pitched squealing, I either turn on a Mariah Carey song or tell my girls to go to bed. Now granted, I don't have a uterus (which my friend Susan pointed out to me one time during a discussion about birth with four other women), but I certainly know females. I live with five of them. That means me and my neutered male dog, Grady, are the minorities. He and I are surrounded by pink stuff everywhere. We like to refer to our house as *Planet Estrogen*, and when we feel we need a shot of testosterone, we escape to the Estro-dome (better known as the basement) to watch *SportsCenter*.

Our house is a place dominated by bright colored bows, glitzy ribbons to match the bows, sweet-smelling lotions that give off the fragrances of mango and cotton candy, fake rhinestone jewelry (from the very popular store for girls, Claire's), and lots of spontaneous crying…I mean *lots*. In fact, if you come by during the day at just the right time you'll hear and see an emotional outburst (sometimes over absolutely nothing). That's just from me. From the girls, it's just about every hour on the hour. Mainly because they can't find any of the clothing that belongs to the hundreds of headless, naked Barbies scattered throughout their rooms. That's something I'll never understand. Not the crying part, but the mystery behind the disappearance of the clothes.

Now when I tell people I have four daughters, men usually say something like, "*Dude*, did you *want* to have four daughters?" I answer, "No, we wanted a hi-def TV." Women say to me, "You need to get in touch with your feminine side." I usually respond with, "How many sides does the 'feminine side' have? Because I've not only been in touch with it; it's actually touched me back."

I love my girls to death—and the beautiful person they came out of: my wife. When they were born, I helped catch all but one, and that's because "the one" was our first of four unmedicated births at home, with a midwife. My wife kept me from catching her because she was applying a satanic-death-grip to my hands, during the delivery process on our bed. I've been involved in their lives from the very beginning and will continue to be involved until the day I die. That involvement will include helping to marry them off to the right men—something that could actually cause me so much stress, I might end up dying because of it. How about that for irony?

So, in order for me to be less stressed, I plan on giving every young man who plans to court my daughters or even thinks about being in the same airspace as them a copy of this book. Not because I'm trying to act like some overprotective intimidator trying to tell young men how to act as husbands to my daughters (that's a given—I know I'll be that for sure). It's because I'm giving away the greatest treasure I have, my daughters, and want to make sure their future husbands are fully prepared to take on the wonderful process of marriage, with my daughters' happiness as the top priority. And why shouldn't it be that way? These are the same young men who may help give me grandchildren one day. I want to make sure they have something I never had when I got married—answers to the thousands of questions they'll be asking themselves about the greatest adventure God ever created: marriage.

To begin, I would want them to know that most of the time women are disappointed in the way we act as husbands. We say dumb things, noises come out of different parts of our bodies, we drool, our hairlines are receding, we're out of shape, we stink, and we have hair on our backs. You try to be married to that, and I promise you, you'll be grossed out. Women don't have hair on their backs, and thank God for that. If they did, wouldn't we still love them? Probably, but certainly electrolysis would be in the picture.

Women are just obviously different. We run yellow lights; they stop. We care about cars; they worry about the cargo in the cars. They can have full-blown conversations with other women while a screaming baby is in the background; we hear a screaming baby and we start to cry ourselves. They can hold a baby while they're eating; we can hardly eat without smearing food on our faces and clothes. They want the children's clothing to match; we're lucky if we can get out the door without clashing. They write legibly; we scribble. They pay attention in church; we fall asleep. They can wear shoes with heels that are three inches off the ground; we can't. They have wallets to go along with the other 50 items in their purses; we have wallets and carry fanny packs. They like to show off the children; we like to show off. They watch soap operas; we watch sports. They "get ready" for bed; we fall asleep on the floor. They like to travel in packs to the restroom; we go by ourselves. They have to wait in line at public restrooms; we don't. They like to lie out by the pool; we do crazy jumps and like to splash people. They like to drink hot tea; we like to grow goatees. They want all the lights in the house on 24/7; we can't turn them off fast enough (or maybe this just happens in my house). Women do lunch; men hang out. They like to drive the speed limit; we like to see if we can beat our own time record when taking road trips. They know the difference between white, eggshell, and beige; we wear black pants with navy blue socks. They worry about whether their butts are too big; we slap each other on the butt and say things like "Atta boy." They reach their sexual peak at thirty-two; we reach our peak at sixteen. They use wet wipes on the kids; we use the bottoms of our shirts. They can blow-dry their hair for hours; we get tired raising our arms for five minutes—either that or we air dry. They want to have dinner in the dining room; we want to have a barbecue. They prefer eye cream; we like ice cream. They smell really good because of their perfume; we always smell like we put on too much cologne. Women can have babies; men act like babies. Their most coveted treasure: jewelry; our most prized possession: the remote control.

Despite our differences, men and women end up doing the exact same things in life, but they just smell better than we do. They're doctors and lawyers, senators and scientists, educators and engineers, athletes and astronauts, judges and sports anchors, computer programmers and presidents of companies. There is just one thing they haven't done yet, and who's to say it won't ever be done? There is a chance that a woman can become president. There is no chance of a man having a baby. So guess what? They're actually one up on us. Plus, as far as keeping pace with us in society's eyes, they have to go through a lot more than we do.

Women are obviously the better occupiers of their time on Earth, but unfortunately, a lot of men just don't want to admit it. For some reason, they're still angry about the whole "Eve ate the apple first and tried to coerce Adam to eat it" thing. They still believe that life is all about them and that's why God made Adam first. Of course, with that type of selfish and illogical thinking, it sometimes leads to a little thing called "alone time," or what some people call "divorce." Since I am not a therapist, I can't explain why some men can't cohabitate with the women they marry. I just know that most of the stuff my wife and I have gone through are experiences we see other couples go through, too. We've fought, argued, yelled, screamed, thrown things, hissed, run away, cried, sucked thumbs, pouted, whined, cringed, and spat. And that was just while I was writing this book.

Despite all of that, we have an understanding that none of that is bigger than our love for each other. Yes, there have been times during arguments that I've wanted to stuff an apple in my wife's mouth and lock her in the pantry. Of course, she's wanted to do the same thing to me, but instead of an apple, it was a grenade, and instead of a closet, it was a pit full of hyenas. I probably deserved it, she probably didn't. Sure, I wish I could act like Jim Duggar, Charles Ingalls, Andy Griffith, Ward Cleaver, or Ozzie Nelson all the time, but sometimes I end up acting like Peter Griffin, Al Bundy, Archie Bunker, and Homer Simpson. Most men do.

Every man encounters a situation in his life when he realizes how awesome his wife is. I knew how awesome my wife was the day she married me. I had no talent, no skill, no top lip, weird hair, and big ears, to go along with an even larger Adam's apple. For you, it could happen at the beginning of marriage, halfway through, or when you're almost dead. It could be so incredible that you have absolutely no words to describe it. Something happens that is so remarkable that you can't stop thinking about it, and you never want to stop talking about it.

I also realized how awesome my wife was when she had our first child at home, in our bed, the all-natural way—without drugs. It was just her, a midwife, a few others, and me. No medication, no doctors, no machines, no insurance forms to fill out, and no hospital restrictions—this was the way women used to do it years ago in the fields of cotton they picked. Back then, though, they would have the baby and then go right back to work in the same fields.

It's the same way today, but obviously the accommodations of where to have a natural birth and the healing process after the birth are a lot more appropriate. Not only did my wife do it once, she did it four times. The last three times around, I was able to play mid-husband and catch the baby when she came out. I was also able to cut the cord, clean her off, and be involved with everything regarding the natural birthing experience. Of course, that was nothing, compared to my wife. She was the superhero, not me. Just as impressive as the baby thing, she's highly educated, she can cook, she's a great mother, she's a certified doula, which means she assists other women in giving birth, and she puts up with me...all the time. Plus, she knows how to spell better than I do.

Anyway, it was the unselfish move of having our children at home that made me realize my life was insignificant compared to hers. All I do is go to work, push a button, and talk to people about sports. Plus, I was able to learn a whole lot more than I expected, about the types of things my wife's body could do.

Up until I married my wife, I really didn't know too much about the inner workings of the female body. I knew enough to get by, but I certainly wasn't ready to enroll in an anatomy class to learn about the biology of my wife's body. I had two sisters, but we never had family chats around the dinner table talking about the physical goings on of their bodies. They usually kept that private. Obviously, a wife is different. She should be able to share information about herself with her husband any time.

Some women may not do this because their husbands are either not interested or think it's weird. I'm glad I know things, because I'm a better husband for it. This is the woman whom I'll spend the rest of my life with, and I genuinely want to know her completely—inside and out.

This isn't a book about the differences between men and women. We know what they are. It's not a book about knowing all the ins and outs of your wife's body, either. This is a book, however, for men who simply want to know three things: 1.) how to make your wife happy after you say or do something stupid; 2.) how to continue doing it until you're both dead, or until you're dead and she remarries a smarter, better-looking, rich guy; and 3.) how to understand everything your wife goes through (physically, mentally, emotionally, spiritually, and financially) and learn to react in a way that's positive for everyone. Basically, be like Dr. Phil, Oprah, Nate Berkus, Dr. Oz, Suze Orman, Ellen, and the cuddly, cute characters from *Sesame Street*, and *not* like Tony Soprano. You can make those three things happen without being too sensitive and without feeling like you're giving up all control. The question is, how sensitive and affectionate should a husband really be toward his wife? That's always been the quandary. You don't want to do things so it seems more like you're her girlfriend than you are her husband. You're not trying to earn an estrogen badge here. But you also don't want to be so manly you do absolutely nothing for her but act like a big jerk.

When it comes to chick flicks, I really don't mind going to see these or staying at home and watching them, either. I don't have a good excuse why; I just like being with my wife, and I know she'll want a shoulder to cry on afterward. I certainly wouldn't go by myself, just like I know she wouldn't watch *Dirty Harry*, *Gladiator*, or *Caddyshack* by herself. Plus, who knows? I might end up earning enough estrogen points for something special *after* the movie. Now some men wouldn't go to chick flicks with their wives, and why they don't, I'll never understand, because we cry in movies all the time. You can deny it all you want, but it's not going to change the fact that we do. Any man who has seen *Brian's Song*, *The Champ*, *Where the Red Fern Grows*, *Old Yeller*, or *My Life* has shed some tears, I promise you that. So if a woman cries in a movie, it's considered a chick flick. If a man cries in a movie, it's considered what, a guy cry? It doesn't necessarily mean we're sensitive or weird for doing it. It just means we thought it was sad. No harm, no foul.

I actually remember the first time I cried in front of my wife. While we were dating, she noticed I had a heavy-haired brow zone, better known as a unibrow or Lee press-on brow. She made mention of it one night, noting that the one brow could be separated into two. I had never really thought about it, but having two separate brows did pique my interest, and I really didn't care to look like Bert from *Sesame Street* anymore. So after the date, we went back to her house and got prepared for the separation. I had no clue what was involved in the process, so I just sat back and relaxed in the recliner. She kept saying, "It's no big deal. It really doesn't hurt." Yeah, right. This was coming from the woman who would one day birth four babies without drugs, at home, in bed. Women should never tell men,

"It doesn't hurt." Everything hurts to us. She then brought in two things: a hot, moist washcloth and a small device she used for her brow area, called tweezers. She told me she would apply the hot rag to the middle of the brow area to moisten the skin and make it easier to pull the hair out. I sat up and said, "Pull the hair out of what?" She replied, "Your nose pad. The part between the eyes." (This is better known as brow fur.) I then asked, "Can't we just shave it or clip it somehow?" She said no, because it was better to get the root of the hair, so it would take a lot longer to grow back.

After hearing how it was done, I wasn't sure if I wanted to go through with it. Up to that point, I had had that patch for nearly twenty-two years of my life. I didn't mind losing it, but I thought I might miss it if it was gone. It had been there through my elementary school years, the weird, traumatic teenage years, through high school football games, proms, and now college. It was just hard for me to let it go. It was my own little personal forehead pet. On the other hand, she had this glowing look on her face like she was about to accomplish one of the greatest tasks in couplehood. It was as if she knew the project (turning me from a frog into Prince Charming) wouldn't be complete unless the unibrow was gone.

I hesitated for a moment and with some slight reserve agreed to do it. She was giddy about it and so excited her hand was shaking. She warmed the spot first and then told me to get ready. She placed the hot rag on my forehead for about ten seconds, and with a quick motion, she reached down and yanked about fifteen hairs and pulled upward. Before I could get a peep out, she then placed the hot rag back on the work area. It was the best slight of hand I had seen in a long while. She did it that fast, hoping I wouldn't notice the pain coming from the nose pad. I was taken aback by her burglar-type moves; I didn't even care how much she robbed from the patch.

She propped the mirror up, and I looked to see the damage. I couldn't believe what I saw. Besides the improvement in my brow area, I observed a small tear falling down my cheek. *What in the?*—I asked myself. This couldn't be what I thought it was, could it? *I'm not crying because of this, am I? It has to be from the damp towel.* I'm embarrassed to say it wasn't. She had pulled so many of my hairs, it triggered a mechanism in my retina area and self-activated the tear duct region, therefore launching the crying sequence. I wasn't doing it on purpose. It just happened, sort of like when someone sneezes three or four times in a row and their eyes get watery. I'll admit, though, it did hurt, and I was very tempted to wail, but I held back.

The point is, your wife probably loves doing stuff with you more than anyone else in the world. If, for some reason, you're more sensitive than the average guy and feel like you shouldn't or wouldn't do some of the stuff she wants you to do, maybe it's time to take a little test before you finish reading this book. The whole point of this book is not to turn into a sweet, sugary muffin who has lost all his masculinity. It's about doing things with and for your wife, and making her happy in the process. If spending time with her watching a movie or improving the way you look by working on a certain body part makes her happy, then by all means do it.

But my masculinity never gets in the way of my wife's femininity. That's rule number one. It shouldn't even have to be a rule. It's a fact. However, there are some men that like doing feminine things, but they just don't realize they're doing them, and if they did, they wouldn't admit it. If you're not quite sure what I'm talking about, the following list will explain. Mark the ones you've done, and then compile your score at the end. This test will not be graded, and only you and your wife will know the results. Place a checkmark next to any statement that is true for you.

- ☐ It takes you longer to do your hair than it takes your wife to do hers.
- ☐ You have had a pedicure or manicure and liked it.
- ☐ You have told another guy his "outfit" looked good.
- ☐ You have talked and cuddled after sex, and actually wanted to.
- ☐ You have cried at a movie that wasn't sports related. (*Old Yeller* doesn't count)
- ☐ You have asked a woman or man if they did something different to their hair.
- ☐ You found yourself thinking more about Valentine's Day than Super Bowl Sunday.
- ☐ You have shaved anything else on your body besides your face.
- ☐ You actually know what "getting in touch with your feminine side" means.
- ☐ You have had a longer conversation about hair products than you had about the type of oil in your car.

☐ You can explain what a dust ruffle is and not a twenty-two belly option.

☐ You know what it means to "color coordinate."

☐ You have been to any of these movies (seen mostly by women and thirteen-year-old girls) and wanted to: *The Notebook*, *Nights of Rodanthe*, *Dear John*, *It's Complicated*, *Valentine's Day*, *27 Dresses*, and any of the *Twilight* and *High School Musical* movies.

☐ You know the lyrics to any boy band song.

☐ You secretly watch shows like *The Bachelorette*, *The Real Housewives of* (insert city), *Oprah*, *Dancing with the Stars*, *Ellen*, or *Rachael Ray*.

☐ You actually know what the Hallmark and Lifetime channels are on your TV.

☐ You recognize these couples' names and know why you do: Bo and Hope, Luke and Laura, Josh and Reva.

☐ You have a tattoo of butterflies, flowers, a unicorn, or a tiger cub.

☐ You've asked your wife, "Do I look okay?" after getting dressed. (Asking, "Do I match?" is okay.)

☐ You listen to songs by Justin Bieber, the Jonas Brothers, and Miley Cyrus and enjoy them, but explain to your friends that your daughter left that music in your car.

Total: _____

If you checked more than half, you may be a little sensitive, but still able to be considered manly. If you checked all of them, you may be a woman and, therefore, instructed to attend a sporting event, scratch yourself like baseball players (or whatever the heck they're doing on live TV for the world to see), growl a few times a day, beat your chest like Tarzan, talk really loud around your coworkers, hunt, fish, wear camouflage, belch, go four-wheeling, buy a truck, dine out at an all-you-can-eat buffet, and speak poor grammar. Because isn't that what all men do anyway?

Okay, so we've established whether you're more sensitive than the average man or not. Does it really matter to your wife, and will it have an affect on the things you do for her to make her happy? Probably not. I'm sure she has accepted you just the way you are and wouldn't care if you were a big ball of mush or hard as a rock. Sensitivity doesn't necessarily mean you have to cry during a chick flick. It just means you're susceptible to your wife's attitudes, feelings, or circumstances.

No matter what kind of people we are, as husbands, our number one priority should be to serve our families—particularly our wives. We should never give the impression that they were put on this planet to look after us. Sometimes, it may unintentionally come across that way, but women need to know that we don't believe that is their purpose. That can be communicated in our words and actions, not only to our wives but to our children also. I know you're not taking your wife for granted. By committing to reading this far, you're already steps ahead of the game than that next guy who seems to be struggling with his relationship more often. Or your wife is making you read it. But if you're like me, you want to grow old with your wife and look back one day and know that you did your very best to make her the happiest woman on the planet. Sometimes we don't make them so happy, and that's when we get burritos to the face.

Listen, we've all heard the saying, "Actions speak louder than words." Let's prove it by using actions and words that help take control of our relationships and make our wives the happiest people on the face of the planet. We might as well. It's their planet anyway, and for now, *it is all about them*.

Chapter Two

Small Brains, Big Mouths

"Only two things are infinite, the universe and human stupidity, and I'm not sure about the former."

—Albert Einstein

D o you remember the dumbest statement you ever made? For me, there are too many instances to name. For my wife, it was May of 1997 in front of hundreds of people. It was just two little words that start with "I" and end with "do," and I think she has regretted saying them ever since.

Now for me, working in radio and TV for eleven years, I've said a lot of dumb things, mostly because of my ADD. One particular time at ESPN Radio, I had to give away two tickets to a Dallas Cowboys game. Now before I continue, I must say that giving away tickets to a Cowboys game in Dallas/Fort Worth is like having Halloween for kids every day. People in Texas love their Dallas Cowboys, just like kids love candy. The ticket giveaway was sponsored by a certain beer company. I should also mention that people in Texas love beer just as much as they love football.

So when I solicited listeners to call in to win the tickets, I mentioned that it was sponsored by *another* beer company, their biggest rivalry in the business. *Big mistake!!!* As soon as I got off the air, my boss called me into his office, wondering why I told three hundred thousand listeners that morning that a certain beer company was giving away tickets, when that certain beer company had no idea, and why the actual beer company that was sponsoring the giveaway wanted me fired for messing up a fifteen-second live commercial read on the air?

In front of my boss, his boss, and the sales manager, I admitted that I screwed up and said that if they wanted to fire me, I would've totally understood. They didn't fire me or kill me, but years later my wife had the chance to do both, because I said the absolute dumbest thing I could've ever said to her.

It occurred in the midst of my wife's sixth month of pregnancy with our first daughter. During a dinner of chicken and dumplings one night, my wife got stressed about not having the right shade of yellow paint in the baby's room. She had a hormonal surge and got upset about what I thought was no big deal. That made me frustrated because I didn't want to see her get irritated over a "little thing" like paint color. (Note: there is no such thing as a "little thing" to a pregnant woman.) I had always heard that if a mother is stressed, the effects of the stress might harm the baby. I didn't know how accurate that information was, so I looked at her and, in a moment of complete boneheadedness, said, "You know, this pregnancy is not all about you." (Meaning that it's also about the baby.)

Now before I continue this story, I should say that right after that moment, I literally saw my life flash before my eyes. Everything was in slow motion after I uttered that damnable sentence. And to make things worse, my mother-in-law was in the room. Also lurking in the house was my father-in-law, who was shaking his head in disbelief at my stupidity.

The reason I tell you this chronicle of my idiocy is so you won't make the same mistake. My wife actually spared my life that night so I could live and be a testament to other men. It is my mission to make sure other men never say those seven little words that came from the laboratory of hell. She looked at me in disbelief, not really thinking I had said what I did. She could have done one of several things to me that night: 1.) She could have taken a rusty steak knife and either cut out my tongue so I would never utter dumb statements again—or cut off my baby-maker so that I could never use that again, for obvious reasons. 2.) She could have called our attorney and filed a restraining order against me. 3.) She could have slapped, punched, kicked, grabbed, pinched, electrocuted, or hit me, but she didn't. She couldn't have then, but now, she could've easily gone to any one of the three hundred fifty thousand mommy blogs that are out there and ripped me to shreds. Instead, she calmly looked at me, put down her fork (thank God), and said to me with some reserve, "What did you just say?" It was as if she was testing me to see how I would respond. I quickly said the universal, all-encompassing word that is used by all men to cover their screw-ups—"nothing"—and continued to eat the wonderful dinner she had made that night.

That's why I wrote this book. I was able to get a do-over. In golf, it's called a mulligan. As grown men, we should be a lot wiser and more in control of what we say, do, think, act, feel, and see, but we're not. We're idiots, and sometimes it takes a while to understand this. But that particular night, I realized one thing (mostly because of the gun my mother-in-law put to my head), and that's this: *It is all about her!* Say it over and over and over and over to yourself until you get it etched into your brain. Before pregnancy, during pregnancy, the delivery, postpartum, and even when the kids are all grown up and moved off, it is and will always be about your wife.

How do I know this? Well, I'm not a doctor, and I don't play one on TV. I'm a sports reporter for a radio station. I get to interview and hang out with some of the greatest athletes in the world. It's a job that's as far away from being a doctor, therapist, psychologist, psychoanalyst, or psychiatrist as it can be. I studied voice diction and took mass media in college—not personality and consciousness. I can't spell Froyed or Soccertease, much less talk about what they thought regarding the human mind. I'm not a marriage counselor, relationship expert, or philosopher, and I don't give professional advice on anything of the sort.

However, I'm an observer. Just like you. I'm someone with personal experience, smart enough to know that women make this world go round. Women do things that men can't even fathom. Their lives are vastly complex and filled with wonder, fascination, and intrigue. They are also simple, loving, kind, generous, meek, and playful. They are the superior beings, and we just haven't admitted it yet.

What makes them superior? Put yourself in the shoes of a woman and try talking on the phone with your mother with one hand while balancing an inexplicably crying two-year-old on the opposite hip. Then gather some dirty laundry with the free arm, carry it to the utility room, place it in the washing machine, and then make sure you mix in the right amount of detergent and put it on the right cycle. You're doing all of this while you're pregnant and with the dog barking at the neighbors. The TV is on in the background blaring a song by a big purple dinosaur,—"I love you, you love me"—and the toilet in the master bedroom just overflowed because your two-year-old thought it would be funny to see if his Buzz Lightyear could actually swim.

The crying gets louder, your mother's asking why you can't keep the baby quiet and offers to come over and help, but you don't want that because the house is a little messy and not up to par with her incredible cleaning standards. There are dishes in the sink, beds to be made, laundry to be picked up, and now you have to call a plumber for the clogged commode. You're placing dry towels down on the tile to soak up the water, you're in your jammies, you haven't even showered yet, you're still holding the crying two-year-old, you ran out of mascara last night, and it's not even 8:00 in the morning yet. Plus, your husband left you the car with no gas. Then you have to add the wet towels that were used to dry the bathroom floor to the ever-growing pile of laundry in the utility room.

Welcome to the life of most mothers. That's not even describing half of what they do, especially women who have another job outside the home. They're zookeepers, potty trainers, taxi drivers, cooks, teachers, counselors, disciplinarians, janitors, hair stylists, carpenters, decorators, jugglers, environmental waste controllers (diaper changers), CEOs of the house, baby beverage makers (breast-feeders), nurses, makeup artists, librarians—and that's just at home with the kids.

This should give you a clearer sense of just how hard, how exasperating, and how never-ending the daily life of a mother really is. On top of that, throw in the fact that their bodies are turned upside down the first time they experience their monthly cycle and until the day they hit menopause. It's a lifetime of swelling, raging hormones and cramps—and that's just on a normal day.

All we have is athlete's foot. They go through all of that, do all the hard work, and we just sit back and enjoy the ride for the most part. We think about cars, sports, movies, sex, and making money. Not necessarily in that order. Family comes in somewhere between God, church, friends, and work. Women are motivated by love, compassion, kindness, loyalty, and shopping for shoes. We're motivated by fantasy football and Madden 11 for our Play Station 3. So, isn't it time to stop griping and start helping with all of that hard work? No? You want to keep griping about having to do extra stuff to help your wife? Okay, then use the phrase I use on my wife when I don't want to do something. When your wife says, "Honey, you want to help me fold these sheets and put up the kids' toys?" you say, "No, I don't want to, but I will anyway." She'll recognize your angst, but appreciate your help. So be mad, but make her happy in the process. You get to pout, while she gets housework done and everyone wins (only if you stop pouting).

150 Secrets to a Happy Wife is not a refresher course in Husbanding 101. It's actually more of a romance reference guide to look at when you're in trouble with your mother-in-law, or at least to act like you're reading when you're in her presence. And one day, if a female friend says, "How do you know what women want or how their bodies function? You don't have a uterus," you can say back to her, "Well, you don't have to be an expert to know that women need help putting the kids to bed and changing diapers after they go through something as serious as birth." That should keep her quiet and make you look like the best husband in the world. It certainly did for me after I was asked that question.

Of course men will never understand what women go through in pregnancy, birth, and delivery, we can never say, "I know what you're going through." However, we can be understanding, have compassion, give a back rub, do the dishes, open the door, fold the laundry, and even do something we're not very good at doing—listen while you talk. But if you ask most women, husbands don't actually do that stuff. The question is, why? This book will explain why and give 150 practical and comical ideas on how to change the "Why?" to "Why in the world would I *not* do any of that to make my wife happier? Of course I would." Unlike those other books with pie charts and graphs, stats, timetables, and long, drawn-out explanations from people smarter than us, *150 Secrets to a Happy Wife* goes more in depth in explaining real-life situations involving the entire family. It basically cuts through the book knowledge and pseudo-intellect, and gets right to the point of describing personal experiences for guys with common sense. Of course, your wife doesn't think you have common sense enough to do any of these things, so that's why you're reading this book. Either that, or you said or did something stupid.

And remember, it's not a book about hunting, fishing, trucks, all-you-can-eat buffets, or war. It's a book about becoming a better husband to your wife, a better father to your children, and a better person overall, after childbirth and beyond. Don't forget, *it's all about them*. (Go ahead and tattoo it on your chest so you won't forget.)

Chapter Three

"I'm Not Fat; I'm Just Big Boned." Nope, You're Fat.

"When I was a young man, I vowed never to marry until I found the ideal woman. Well, I found her, but alas, she was waiting for the ideal man."

—Henri Alain-Fournier, French essayist and philosopher

B efore we can move forward, we need to look backward from where we came. Remember life before you and your wife had a baby? Sex, sex, and tons of sex, along with eating, sleeping, working, eating, sleeping, dates, adventure, romance, more eating, vacations, work, romance, and excitement. Wasn't that the life? Things seemed so simple because they were worth the effort and all the time and energy. Plus, you were younger. That could have been years ago or just recently. In fact, if you just had a baby, you may feel a lot older than you did in the recent past.

What about now? The baby has arrived and is growing or grown. There's more of the work, but less of the romance, excitement, and adventure. Why do you think that is? Less interest? Less time? Less trying? Probably all of the above. The adventure is actually still there, but the scenarios are different.

Who is the one that stopped all of the dates, adventure, excitement, and romance? Was it you or your wife? Odds are that you stopped it and concentrated more on the eating, work-ing, sleeping, and playing. She's always expected the other stuff because you did it before you had kids, but now everything's different. She still craves your attention and affection, but maybe in the form of talking and listening and not necessarily with groping and grabbing.

The question is, why is it different? Why did you stop doing the things you did before, like taking out the trash without being asked, doing the dishes, helping with dinner, telling her you love her, going out on dates, and treating her with respect in public? Is it because you had kids? Maybe her body changed. What if your body changed? Maybe the romance is dead. Maybe your wife had postpartum depression and never recovered. Whether these are some of the reasons, or whether you have a newborn or little Johnny is in his forties, this book gives you plenty of ideas on how to make your wife's life better and continue to do so the rest of her life. And I speak from experience; making your wife's life better has a direct impact on the quality of your own life. You'll basically be able to do whatever you want. It doesn't mat-ter if it's the first year of marriage, the third year, the seven-year itch, or the golden fiftieth.

So let's get focused and figure out why and when the relation-ship may have gone from "I do" to "I don't," as in, "I don't have to listen to my wife," "I don't have time to play with my kids; that's my wife's job," or even, "I don't have to help around the house; I do enough at work." Obviously, those ideas aren't going to help you get back on track and in true form—and they're not very popular among women, either. So the question is, "What are the best things to say and do, and when is the right time they should be said and done?" I'm glad you asked, because in order to answer that question, you need to understand what women go through when they find out they're pregnant.

You need to actually sit in the driver's seat the entire nine months of physical, spiritual, financial, and mental change, from start to finish. This means executing the same motions and range of emotions that they encounter after the delivery, the next day, two weeks after, a month down the line, a year from that point, and every minute of every hour of every day after that, not stopping until you truly know the differences between what they feel and what men feel. Of course, you still won't be able to even get close to how it really is for women. That's okay, though, because you're not supposed to know how it is. You're a man. You won't ever know how it is. What you do after your baby is born will truly define what level you're on. So we start with the questions all women want to ask. What would happen if men were able to get pregnant? How would it really be?

You, this pregnant man, probably wake up one morning really late and realize you overslept by accident. You check your alarm and notice you didn't hear it go off. You want to skip work and sleep the entire day. You literally have to take naps to recover from taking naps—you're that tired. You wonder if you need more iron or need to start going to bed earlier. You get up the next morning, still tired, and fix yourself some breakfast. It doesn't matter what it is, after you get it down your throat, you throw it right up.

Suddenly, you're nauseated. Unfortunately though, while you

were busy vomiting, you got some of it on your shirt. That causes you to get a little emotional and do something you haven't done in a while. Your tear ducts actually unleash some wet, watery, gushy stuff that streams down your cheek. You start to wonder, "Is it hair gel dripping down from my scalp?" "Is there a hole in the roof causing the ceiling to leak?" No. It's called crying. You're curious why you're doing it, because the last time you can recall crying was when you were six years old. You're feeling really vulnerable at that moment and contemplate staying home, but realize you have to go to work. You dry your eyes and head out the door.

As soon as you get to work, you make a beeline for the men's room. For some reason lately, you've been going a lot more often than usual. While you're there, you unload some more breakfast. That's strange, because you're also salivating over the donut smell coming from the break room. You follow the trail of donut odor to grab some Krispy Kremes. While heading for the break room, you wonder why your nipples are feeling sensitive and tender. Could it have been the rough fabric of the shirt you put on after you threw up earlier at your apartment? Could it be the new biodegradable soap you used when you washed your clothes? You pass it off as being weird and go to your office. On your way there, you hug every person you come in contact with. You actually start crying again but get in your office before anyone sees you doing it. You're trying to figure out why you're so overwhelmed at being at work and chalk it up to emotional dysfunction. You sit at your desk and wonder if you should call the doctor to find out if you're coming down with something.

Come lunchtime, you head for the doctor's office, only to wait in the lobby for forty-five minutes once you get there. You look around for magazines and notice the most current issue of any "guy" magazine is two years old. That frustrates you enough to make you start crying again. You look around for a tissue or at least a female magazine with relevant articles that's not outdated. By the time you finally find a magazine, the nurse calls you back into the examining room. You put on the "air-conditioned" robe and take a seat on the crackly butcher paper, waiting anxiously for the doctor's arrival. You start to wonder why they ever started using butcher paper on an examining table, which reminds you of the deli down the street that has great sub sandwiches and garlic pickles. They use the same paper. You start to get hungry again.

A female doctor comes in and checks your symptoms, asks you to urinate in a cup, takes your blood pressure, and goes to her office. She comes back to let you know that you're not coming down with the latest virus. You're happy about that but still curious why all the other stuff is happening. You tell her you're experiencing fatigue, frequent urination, nausea, sensitive breasts, sensitivity to smell, food aversions, change of skin, mood swings, and you feel like you're losing control of your body. She then gives you a high five and congratulates you. You're asking her why, and she gives you a "you gotta be kidding me" smile and says, "This is the beginning stage of pregnancy, young man." Time to call your parents and spread the good news because nine months will be here before you know it. Better make that the weird news instead of the good news. Of course, while she's telling you that, she's also doing a check-up (most women get their check-ups from male doctors).

All of a sudden, 1,001 thoughts rush through your head. Your life has officially changed. No more softball games with the team at work, no more flag football on Saturdays, and no more hanging out with the guys playing Wii till 2:00 in morning. However, karaoke night on Tuesday with the guys from accounting is okay. One day, you'll look in the mirror and notice that the thirty-four-inch waistline has disappeared. You'll look down and notice you went from six-pack abs to a keg. No more whistles, no more stares, no more admiring glances, and no more double takes. Just a lot of waddling in your running shorts. Not necessarily a pretty sight, especially now that your buns of steel are morphing into a nice, thick lump of cellulite growing underneath your buttocks region. Add that to the fact that your skin is breaking out, your eyes are red-rimmed from being so weepy, and your face looks pasty and pale. You can't stop craving fried bologna and mayonnaise sandwiches, and you can't stop hurling them back up. Your back hurts, and you're exhausted. You have to go buy new clothes, but no one will go with you, which gives you another reason to cry. You can't wear what you used to, and now you're contemplating doing something different with your hair. No reason, just because. Maybe highlights, maybe lowlights, maybe even a buzz cut—you just aren't sure.

The months pass, and now you're "showing." That means your gut is sticking out for the world to see, including your friends and coworkers. They think you're eating too much and are wondering why the weight is accumulating only in the stomach region. You don't say a word about being pregnant, and you tell them you've been eating and drinking a lot of food and beverages with very high sodium content. They buy the explanation but still don't understand why you allow all the women at work to touch your stomach.

Your apartment has turned into a nursery. At one time, you hosted Monday Night Football, but now you're hosting Wednesday night prenatal yoga classes. You find yourself pondering baby names all the time. You catch yourself writing down first, middle, and last name combinations during staff meetings while Bob is explaining the last quarter's earnings. Then there's the whole issue of baby name styles. "Should I go with a cool, hip, popular name or keep it simple and classic? What if it's a boy and not a girl, or vice versa?"

Feels weird, doesn't it? Of course it feels weird to a guy. We're not designed to experience pregnancy. We could never pull off something of that magnitude and still have the patience for it, the time, the brains, the sensitivity, the love, or the care. We get emotional when we find out we have to get a rectal exam. We would obviously freak out if a doctor told us we were expecting a baby. The physical exams alone would be one hundred times worse than a plain old rectal. There's prodding and poking involved at a much higher degree. The stress level would be at an all-time high. Just being in a mother's shoes for one instant and describing everything in detail scares us. I remember how weird it was watching the movie *Junior* with Arnold Schwarzenegger and Danny DeVito. They made a man having a baby look very real and plausible. I know that's just Hollywood, but it was frightening to have that image in my mind.

That's why God chose women to have babies and not men. However, he didn't intend for them to do it on their own or try to recuperate by themselves afterward.

That's where the secrets-to-making-your-wife-happy part comes into play for you. It's understanding what your wife experiences and devoting every last breath and every ounce of energy to making sure she has a prosperous and healthy recovery. That means saying and doing the right things and showing some major patience through what we usually show dogs and cats all the time: unconditional love. Of course, our wives aren't ten-pound furballs and don't purr. What you're offering is unselfish acts of kindness all the time. Not questioning or complaining ever. It's a love that says, "You, my wife, gave all of yourself through the act of incubating our child for nine months in his first apartment and expelling him in the most dramatic way possible. In return, I'll prop your pillows, make you breakfast, and take the kids to school. Then we're even."

Okay, maybe you're not even, but what you've done is make the recovery process a lot smoother and a lot more comfortable for your wife due to your servanthood. You've also set a precedent and a pattern for how you'll behave from that point on. It would be very egotistical to make a big deal out of thinking you changed to make yourself look better, but that's why we're doing this in the first place. However, she'll definitely notice the new direction you're moving in and probably acknowledge it in a rewarding fashion.

Remember, mothers, mothers-in-laws, nannies, and even full-time servants are great. But they're not you. They're not her soulmate. They leave after the baby is born, when the "baby-moon" is over and all the newness has worn off. You're the one who gets to stick around and watch all of the drama, tears, laughter, and body changes. So, you have two choices: 1.) you can be a lump of dough and just sit around and do absolutely nothing, or 2.) you can jump right in to the mix of things and be involved with everything.

If you chose the latter, good for you. Be prepared to not only help your wife but also help yourself. Your actions, behaviors, and the way you honor your wife are relative to the result you get back from her. In man-speak, it means if you're nice to her, she's probably going to be nice to you. Being nice can mean much more than just giving your wife a back massage or cleaning the house or preparing her favorite blueberry waffles with maple syrup. It could also mean that your actions toward her, around her, and for her will contribute to the welfare of her recovery and to your life together. If your kids are mostly grown up, don't think that your wife doesn't need that same unconditional love, nurturing, and attention. News flash: she does, and she probably needs it a lot more often.

Now, since this book is all about your wife and not you, we'll start with some of the basic fundamental ideas on how you can begin or continue romancing her. These are simple things that take zero time to execute. They sort of coincide with each other and work toward accomplishing the same goal: making your wife happy. They may not be very popular with you, and I'm sure they've been mentioned a time or two in the past hour, day, week, month, year, and lifetime, but if you grasp these, there's no doubt you'll be able to do the rest of the suggestions with ease. And just in case you've already forgotten, *it's all about her*.

It's all about her idea #1: Do the dishes

Have you seen dishwashers today? They're like cars without wheels—they literally do everything. They're computerized, they talk, they have lights and buttons and other things you have to read a manual to learn about. Master this, and your wife will probably be your love slave for the rest of your life. This is the ultimate aphrodisiac for women. Forget tropical islands with white sandy beaches, that trip to Paris, a new red convertible, millions of dollars worth of jewels, and good looks. (Well, maybe not the jewels, because women really love jewelry.) Those things are nice and certainly worth marrying for, but if you are willing to do this any, all, or most of the time, forget about the other things. You won't need them. The question is, do you know how to do the dishes? Don't say no just to get out of it. You can basically do it after any meal by wiping the food off the plate, putting the dish in the dishwasher (that's that thing by the sink that makes a loud noise), putting soap in the open contraption, closing the door, and pushing "start." It's that simple. If the washer is broken, just do them by hand.

Secret to success for pre-washing the dishes by hand: the major point in this is to wipe everything off the plate. You don't want to put a plate in the machine with chunks of food hanging off it. The way to head that off is to wipe the plate after you use it, before you ever get to the point of doing the dishes. That goes for dishes from breakfast, dinner the night before, or even three days ago. Of course, if three days go by with dishes still in the sink, that either means your wife is on her deathbed or she hasn't walked by the sink and noticed the pile of dishes. Women are more susceptible to untidiness than men are.

It's all about her idea #2: Do the laundry

Do you want your wife to be your love goddess the rest of your life? Then master this idea. Believe it or not, this is probably the biggest chore your wife has on her cleaning list. It's a never-ending cycle of clothes getting cleaned, people wearing the clothes, clothes getting dirty, and then clothes needing to get cleaned again. It never ends. Your wife has to put your dirty socks, underwear, t-shirts, and pants in the washer all the time. You look and smell fresh and clean because she does it every day. It feels good to have clean drawers on doesn't it? You can thank your wife for that. Say thank you by doing it yourself every once in a while. Not just your stuff—throw in a towel or two. Make sure you know how to do it. It's not rocket science, but you don't want to explain your shell pink underwear to the other guys at the gym.

It's all about her idea #3: Don't object to her getting her hair done

How many women do you known who shave their heads ON PURPOSE? Probably not too many. Women don't get buzz cuts or mohawks just for the fun of it like men do. Men spend money on cars, video games, sporting events, TV stuff, and movies. Women spend money on hair, hair products, hair extensions, hair lotions, hairsprays, hair gels, haircuts, hair removal, and hair color. Think about why your wife is stronger than you. Take the time she spends washing, conditioning, and blow-drying her hair, multiply that by the time her arms move up and down, and it equals very strong muscles. She needs a break from this. If you ever really listen to women when they meet for lunch or see each other after a long time, you'll notice there are two things they talk about most. War and politics? No! Stocks and bonds? No! Fantasy football and movies? Not those either. They love their hair. Next to their faith and children, they talk about hair more than anything. In fact, next to the children, your wife's hair is her pride and joy. Believe that or not, it's true. They curl it, spray it, color it, straighten it, tease it, cut it, blow-dry it, and sometimes they hate it. We're just happy if ours is still on our head.

Think back to all of the engagements you've missed over the years because she didn't like the way her hair looked. I bet there have been quite a few. Some you cared about; others you were glad you missed (weddings and showers). If she can get by with blaming the stylist who messed up her hairdo, so be it. It's like you watching sports—it's your passion in life. Women love getting their hair done—it's their passion. Granted, even if she goes to a stylist, she still may not be happy with the result. It doesn't matter. Oh, and don't try to compliment her on her hair either. It doesn't matter what you say, she'll still change it (although you are likely to score a few points if you at least notice that her hair has changed).

When a woman is sick of dealing with her hair (which will happen often), one thing that may help her is if you brushed it. Word is that a man brushing his wife's hair was very popular in the seventies and is making a huge comeback. It will not only help give her arms a rest, but it will also be a treat for your wife to know you're getting all the tangles out. You can use a soft brush, put some romantic music on, turn the lights down, and use long, slow strokes. You could even pretend you're her stylist, "Sebastian." While you're at it, give her a little scalp massage. If she's bald, just go with the scalp massage.

It's all about her idea #4: Remember the most important days: Mother's Day, her birthday, Valentine's Day, your wedding anniversary

You can remember the score from the 2003 Division Three Women's Softball National Championship between Irrelevant University and Not Important College, but you can't remember your wife's birthday? Well thank God for Facebook, because there's actually a reminder on the right side of the main page that informs you of this important date. And shouldn't these dates be common knowledge? For goodness sake, some of the important ones are written on the calendar every year for us. Don't make it harder than it is. Granted, there are a ton of dates we have to remember: kids' birthdays, parents' birthdays, in-laws' birthdays, but the four dates that are the most important are the ones that honor your wife: Valentine's Day, Mother's Day, her birthday, and your wedding anniversary. If you happen to forget your father-in-law's birthday, I'm sure he won't mind. If you forget to celebrate Arbor Day, I'm sure it won't be a problem. If you don't send a card on your parents' anniversary, I'm sure they'll forgive you.

But if you forget her birthday, Mother's Day, Valentine's Day, or your anniversary, you may be in a little trouble. One day was the most important to your wife, in front of a lot of people and God. Another is celebrated by couples all over the planet, who spend billions of dollars on chocolate, balloons, cards, and teddy bears. She expects you to be a part of that. And the other day not only gives homage to your wife but also to your mother.

You should remember to begin preparation more than twenty-four hours before the event. Remember, though, for obvious reasons, that your wife and mother are not equal.

It's all about her idea #5: Actually pay attention to what she is saying

The more children you have, the harder this gets. Plus, if you have ADD, you're really going to have a hard time doing this. Put the paper down, turn the sports off, and listen to what your wife is actually saying. If your wife has ever said, "I've said it four times already; can you not hear me?" and you replied, "Yes, but the first three times I really wasn't listening," this one's for you. Don't just hear noise coming from the opposite side of the room. Your wife wants to have a deep conversation and needs your undivided attention. Maybe it's not deep, but she wants you to listen anyway. Whether it's when you arrive home from work, at night in bed, or when you go out to eat by yourselves, pay attention to what she's saying so you can have an intelligent response. She may have been talking with kids all day.

Help her look forward to seeing you each evening by listening intently to her day's events before sharing yours. She wants to feel like she's connecting with you. If she doesn't do it with you, she'll find someone else to connect with, like her mother. That means your mother-in-law will be wondering why her daughter is talking to her about her day and not to you. Quick fix: just listen to her and let her share her thoughts. It may take five minutes or fifty-five minutes. You won't know until you do it. Either that, or get another job to pay for the phone bill.

By the way, you may want to stay in one spot while she's talking. I know I sometimes like to walk around and give her the excuse, "I'm listening; go ahead." That's not going to work. She wants your undivided attention.

It's all about her idea #6: Change a diaper (only if still relevant)

Yes, some of what is produced in diapers from our sweet, precious little angels of gooeyness smells like something straight out of hell itself. However, it's common knowledge that for at least the first year of childhood, children cry because of a few things. They're either hungry, tired, hurt, or they have a dirty diaper. One can usually deduce whether a kid is hungry from the time of day. If a kid is tired, he or she will usually fall asleep or start to moan very loudly. If a kid is hurt, none of the solutions for hunger, sleep, or diaper change will offer any relief. If a kid has a bad diaper, you'll probably be able to smell it from anywhere in the house. Either that, or you'll smell toxic fumes coming from underneath their door. Just follow your nose and you'll find your child. A dirty diaper could mean one of two things: pee pee or poo poo. Don't ever get grossed out in front of your wife and say things like, "I can't believe I'm doing this," or "Will you come help me?" You're not going to get any sympathy from her. She does this all day long. Besides, this is your own flesh and blood. You are at least half-responsible for the producer of these waste elements existing, so it is only logical that you be at least half-responsible for cleaning him or her up. Quit worrying that the kid's poo reminds you of the green stuff you've seen in movies like *Alien*—think unconditional love. Remember, they just do it for a few years and then they're potty trained. Your diapers may have to get changed when you're about ninety years old, so make sure you change theirs without complaining.

It's all about her idea #7: Ask her what she wants in the bedroom

And it's not food and sports mixed with sex, as we discussed earlier. It's more like a new concept—pleasing her for once. Never heard of this? This means no more two-minute drill. Keep that where it belongs—in football. You rush through everything else in life; don't do it here. This isn't supposed to be fast food.

It's set up to be more like a full-course meal, with foreplay as the appetizer. I'm not a sex therapist, so I won't begin to try to explain in full detail what this means, but let's just say you'll have to get rid of all selfishness during sex. I know this may be a new concept, but if you do this, you'll become the greatest love machine of all time. But it also means you'll have to start things off slow, Mr. "I jump into sex way too fast and don't have time for her emotional intimacy." This could mean some touching and kissing combined with some talking, whispering, cuddling, and hugging, maybe even a bubble bath.

It's sort of like the fable we all read in grade school. Okay, I didn't actually read it, but I know someone who did. It's the tale of the tortoise and the hare. We're the rabbits; they're the turtles; the speeders versus the crawlers. Change your style and become less of a speeder and more of a crawler, and I bet the results will be rewarding. Plus, she'll stop using the headache excuse over and over again. Insider's secret: Your behavior and actions are directly proportional to the amount of affection or action you'll receive. If you don't like what you are receiving from your wife, change what you are giving.

It's all about her idea #8: Defend her in front of your mother

If you're a self-proclaimed mama's boy, you might want to read this. Or if you stick up for your mom in arguments against your wife (and you're still alive to talk about it—and still married), this one's for you.

Norman Bates probably would have been a better person if he'd only gotten out from under the shadow of his decrepit, dead, and decomposing mother. Instead, he let her kill any chances of him having a relationship with any woman. Don't let yours do the same. Mothers are awesome, and I love mine dearly, but don't ever take her side against your wife. First of all, you shouldn't have to, and secondly, it's never a good idea. While you're at it, don't ever talk badly about your wife in front of your mother and family members. It makes you look like you're a miserable husband stuck in a marriage you can't get out of, and it validates any negative ideas they have about your wife. (These comments will come back to haunt you later—guaranteed.) If you have anything to say to your wife, say it to her in private.

It's all about her idea #9: Don't ever compare schedules

If your wife sits at home all day and does absolutely nothing, then go for it. Compare schedules all you want. If not, I would never do this. The words "Boy, I've have a hard day" don't really resonate with women, especially if they come out of a man's mouth right when he gets home from work. When you say that, you're basically saying that your wife's daily duties are secondary compared to yours, especially when you don't ask her how her day has been. You're saying she has the second-hardest schedule in the family. For all we know, you could sit at a desk all day and type. That's not hard work. Neither is talking on the phone, filing papers, or computing.

Have deadlines at work or think you have stress? Take a three-year-old to Chuck E. Cheese for a few hours, and you'll experience real stress. Try to comfort a baby when he has an ear infection at 3:00 in the morning. Try to blow-dry the hair of a two-year old or trim his nails. We'll see how much you get done while he's squirming. You're in a cushy office with stimulating people, air-conditioning, a comfortable chair, restrooms, adult conversation, a water fountain, and a snack room.

Now, if you're a ditch digger, someone who lays tar in 105-degree heat, a soldier on active duty, a welder in Arizona, an NFL football player, an off-shore oil rig driller, or a coal miner, your job might be harder than your wife's. Okay, you guys are excluded. If you want to say anything, say you both work hard. It may not seem like it, but some women feel unappreciated and invalidated when they hear their husbands implying they work harder than them.

It's all about her idea #10: Clean parts of the house

Grab a toilet brush, get some cleaner, and erase that filthy toilet ring around the john. Maybe it's been there forever, and you may have even contributed to it the most. It doesn't matter, because your wife has her hands full. You use the restroom the same amount she does, so if you mess something up, help her out and clean it up. Why wait for your wife to dust the shelves, vacuum a room, or clean a smudge from a window or mirror? Haven't you ever heard of Mr. Clean? He's the bald guy with the loop earring on the front of the cleaning product your wife uses. He's not ashamed of cleaning, so why should you be? If you can make time to help with the little things, no doubt she'll repay your effort. We know she can handle the big things. She had your baby, after all. That's a huge deal. Mopping a kitchen floor, an area that's about one hundred square feet, shouldn't be a big deal for you. By the way, this isn't a once-a-month endeavor—regular mopping is what we are aiming for here.

It's all about her idea #11: Wear your wedding ring—all the time

If you want women to think you're single, continue to not wear it. Of course, then, you'll have to keep making up excuses for why you don't wear it: "I work with my hands, so it gets in the way," "I was working out and lifting those weights with a ring on is hard to do," or the one I used to use, "I can't wear it at night when I sleep, it bugs me ." One year or fifty years, it really doesn't matter how long you've been married. You should never have to take it off unless you're dead. Some men actually feel no difference between marriage and death, but certainly not me. Quit using the excuse that you have to take it off at the gym because of the weights, or that you're on the computer all day, or that you're sleeping, or that you are doing yard work. That doesn't matter to your wife. She probably wears hers 90 percent of the time.

There are actually some women out there that may find you attractive. If they see you without a ring on, they may make a move. You don't need to give women an excuse to make a move on you. Skip the hassle and temptation and just keep your ring on. It's not only the symbol that says you're off the market; it also signifies your love and commitment to your wife. Plus, if you take it off all the time, you may end up literally paying dearly for it. I did. I lost mine.

It's all about her idea #12: Make an effort to get along with her (GULP) mother

Unless your name is Adam, and you didn't have one of these because you were married to Eve, all men—kings, presidents, doctors, athletes, and even therapists—have to go through the same trials you do. Not all men hate their mother-in-laws. I love mine so much and hope she reads this part. Your mother-in-law is the lifeline to your wife. If it weren't for her, you wouldn't have your wife. Sure, you may not have been the first choice for her daughter, and she may still call you Chet when your name is Chad, but remember, she's still the grandmother of your kids. She's also the one who will decide who gets what in the inheritance.

Look at it this way, you know you're going to see her at least a few times a year for Thanksgiving and Christmas, depending on how many kids you have and where she lives. Even if your mother-in-law hates you, love your wife by showing her that you're trying to get along with her mother, and always treat her with respect. If you want to, just pretend you're the United States and she's France. You really don't have to get along, and you may not agree with her stance on some issues, but to keep the peace among the people, you're both diplomatic when needed. And although France says she's your ally, she may still say some nasty stuff about you behind your back. Don't worry about it. Just keep telling yourself you're bigger than she is and you can stop the importing and exporting of goods anytime you want (this means shipping the grandkids off to her place and back). Of course, I don't know this from personal experience. My mother-in-law is great!

It's all about her idea #13: Don't ever force her to recover faster from birth

Let's cut open your abdomen and remove something that weighs nine pounds, and we'll see how fast you can recover from major surgery. I dedicate this one to my friend Dean. He actually had the gall to ask his wife when she was going to "clean the house" eight days after she had a C-section (this is when the doctor cuts open a woman's abdomen and uterus to remove the baby). Yes, he's still married, but he was stripped of all bedroom rights for at least a year. The average recovery a woman should have after giving birth is six weeks to three months, probably more if she's been cut due to an episiotomy or a C-section. Don't assume that just because she's home, she's ready to jump right in and do all of the housekeeping again. In other words, let her decide when and how much she's going to do. By rushing her, you may just push her right into postpartum depression (this happens in the period after birth) or push her right to a divorce attorney. Some authorities on birth will tell you that the actual process of birth is equal to a fifty-mile hike. Go run that, and we'll start the clock afterward to see how much rest you need.

Let the recovery run its course, and don't say something stupid that's going to get you on the couch at bedtime. Believe me, the baby's crying at 3:00 in the morning may do that anyway.

It's all about her idea #14: Don't object to her going back to work

This one's for all the male chauvinists out there who still think it's cool to act like you're in control of your wife. Wake up, Mr. Barbarian. This is the twenty-first century. You don't rule your wife, and you shouldn't run her life. Everyone knows that except you. Now more than ever, your wife and women in general are doing stuff that makes you look like you're still in the dark ages. She's having babies. She's organizing and planning your life, her life, and your kids' lives. She's the head of a company. She's an astronaut. She's a professor. She's a doctor, an attorney, an engineer, and, most importantly, the mother of your children. This isn't the age of "barefoot and pregnant" anymore. It's more like "barefoot, pregnant, and back to work." If a woman wants to go back to work after the birth of her baby, she should always have that option. If she decides that it's not for her, that's okay, too—the key is that it should be her decision.

Some men don't want their wives to work because they may make more money or be more successful. On the other hand, other men don't mind their wives working because they want her to spend her own money on the things she wants and needs. That's another issue for another day, but whatever the reason, it's very played out and very unpopular. Just because your circle of friends may act this way, doesn't mean you should. Your wife isn't looking for a dictator or a boss. She's looking for a loving partner. She wants someone who will work to build a happy and quality life with her, not someone who's going to dictate her every move.

It's all about her idea #15: Look groomed

Unless you're name is Mike Rowe, and you're the host of a show called *Dirty Jobs* (on the Discovery channel) or someone with a dirty job, this one's for you. Whether it's dirt under the nails, a unibrow, nose or ear hair, or smelly socks, you may not look like the sharp young man she married years ago—and you need to. For some reason, you've decided to let yourself go almost too far toward looking like a Neanderthal. Congrats, you've taken all the attraction you once had and chucked it down the tubes. That's okay, because your wife loves you unconditionally. Now go trim the hair, wax the back, brush the teeth, lose the paunch, and give the trucker hat to Goodwill. Oh, and make sure you get that little patch of hair on the Adam's apple. Men always seem to miss that and the part directly under the nose, too.

Chapter Four

HELP! My Husband Looks Like Shrek

"It is not good for the man to be alone.
I will make a helper suitable for him."

—Genesis 2:18, *The New International Bible*

If you're a man who's proud of having love handles, slouching shoulders, a five o'clock shadow at other times of the days besides five o'clock, bad breath, ear hair, and grease under the nails, skip this chapter. Evidently, you don't care anymore about your appearance, so this chapter might not do you any good. As men, we're sometimes vulgar, gross, sloppy, slow-witted, pigheaded, uncultured, uncouth, uneducated, ill-tempered, inconsiderate, unkempt, and irresponsible. That was just the list from yesterday. Sometimes the list gets better. Often it gets worse and longer. The project your wife undertook to evolve you into a well-respected father, businessman, husband, and gentleman may have lost its luster. Right now, you're still a self-involved ingrate highly motivated by nothing more than food, sports, and sex. Maybe it was all an act before you got married? Did your wife fall in love with Romeo and end up with Bubba? Should there have been a sticker that said, "Thirty-day money back guarantee," or "Some assembly required"? Maybe so. That's why this second list of tips offers a tune-up to help you be your best around your wife and children. Consider it an overhaul.

It's like when you gain a few pounds; the first thing that comes to mind is how you're going to work them off. You join a gym and get back in shape. Unless you're an undernourished international model, this cycle happens to the best of us. Eat, gain weight, complain about gaining weight, work out, lose weight, and eat again. It's the same thing with being a husband and father. We're good, then bad, good again, bad again, and then good. We have to always stay in shape—physically, mentally, spiritually, and financially. Of course, being married also takes a toll on you emotionally, but then add kids to the mix, and you *really* have to be in shape emotionally. You may be out of shape right now in all categories and need a domestic workout. This is where we start: the basic training.

Did you know more money is being spent on weight loss gimmicks today than any other time in the history of the United States, but we're still the fattest we've ever been? Here's another interesting stat: more products that remove body hair are being bought than ever before. How about that? We're fatter, hairier, and evidently broke, because we're spending all of our money on products we're not using.

This is a wake-up call. Remember, there was a time when men were perfect, so in this chapter, we explore the reprogramming we need as a result of being born into the male species. We need to find out when things went south for the entire male species, not just you. Somewhere in the past six thousand years something went terribly wrong, and at some point, man became just like the wild beasts of the jungle.

If you ask theologians, some will suggest it started in the beginning, when God made Adam. It didn't take God too long to realize Adam needed some help. He lived all by himself in this luscious garden that was beautifully landscaped, but he needed more than just the fruit trees and animals. He needed something or someone to help keep the garden looking manicured at all times, so that when visitors came over, it wouldn't look like a frat house. He also needed someone to feed the animals, because we know men aren't good at taking care of pets, and we aren't good at yard work either. He needed a woman's touch. So God made woman.

Her name was Eve. This may or may not be biblically accurate, but word is that when Adam saw Eve for the first time, he said to God, "Whoa, man!" God then responded, "That's right, Adam. She is a 'whoa, man,' but it's actually pronounced 'woman.' I'm giving her to you because within the last few days, you've gone from keeper of the garden to lonely naked guy talking to the animals."

That's the funny thing about Adam and Eve. After God made Adam, He then made Eve. Maybe. He had to make her because he felt sorry for Adam? Did God know that man couldn't live without woman, or was He using the old adage, "Practice makes perfect" and then realized he got it right the second time? After all, He made Adam from the dust of the earth and said, "This guy needs a companion." Then He made Eve from Adam and afterward said, "Everything is good."

Think about that. Men were made from dirt. That's how much God thought of us. He obviously thought more of Eve because she was designed differently from Adam. I'm not God's personal publicist, but if I were a betting man, I bet He probably gave Adam a once-over and thought, "Hmmmm...not quite what I imagined. Let's see, if I take a rib from his rib cage, I wonder what will happen." Eve happened, and therefore all women happened. Since that day, mankind (for this book's sake, maybe we should use *womankind*) hasn't been the same. Planet Earth has dramatically changed.

So what does that mean for you now? It means that your wife is a wonderful creation and should be respected in that way. Of course, you are also a wonderful creation, but obviously God didn't intend to make men and women alike. The plan from day one was to see how two different people could coexist in the most wonderful place on the planet, find a starting point, and build from there. Obviously, things have changed since Adam and Eve. Change can be a good or bad thing. It just depends on whom you ask and what the situation is. So the big questions for this chapter are "How different are you and your wife now (since marriage)?" and "How have you adapted to change in your own relationship?"

First of all, your wife's name changed; yours didn't. That was an easy one. Looking at the overall, big picture, I would venture to say that women, in general, adapt more easily than men. Ever move to another state fourteen hours away from your friends and family? See how fast a woman takes charge of getting things done? It's pretty fast. Once she's in that new state, she starts adapting rather quickly. She changed homes, friends, jobs, and everything else, just like that. Why do you think women are always doing their hair differently? Once you start getting comfortable with the way it looks, your wife goes out and cuts it all off. They don't plan this; they don't ask you about it (they never do and don't have to). Sometimes, in an impulse situation, they just go do it—they don't tell the other women in the neighborhood and they certainly don't tell their moms. They just have it done without any consultation. Which again, is fine. They want change—they get change. It's that simple.

We, on the other hand, have a hard time changing our underwear from day to day. We like comfort more than inconvenience. Changing is inconvenient for us. It's just difficult parting with a nice, soft pair of boxers. It's also hard for us to get rid of any of our other pieces of clothing. You could probably pick out a jacket, a shirt, a hat, a coat, some shoes, or even a bunch of ties your wife has tried to throw away a hundred times, but for some reason they're still around. You've managed to keep them hidden from clothes purgatory, a place your wife has been many times. She actually calls it the garbage, but in her head she thinks of it as a place where old, worn-out pieces of clothing go to burn and never be seen again.

If women could change what's in their closet every week, they would do it in a heartbeat. Why do you think they change outfits twenty times before you go anywhere? Then they ask you those dreaded questions: "Do I look fat in this?" "Does this make me look hippy?" (not referring to the seventies but wondering if her hips look big), "Do these shoes match these earrings?" It doesn't matter what you say. They're going to change again anyway.

What about at a restaurant? You sit down, you peruse the menu, everyone has settled on what they're ready to order, the waiter comes over to your table, and all of a sudden you hear,

"Take their orders first; I'm still looking," Your wife changes her order. First she wanted a salad, then soup and salad, then the chicken salad. She couldn't make up her mind. You kept it simple and went with the steak.

One of the biggest changes I always have to deal with is the fact that my wife wants to change something about the interior design of our house every month. "We need to paint that wall a different color," she says. "Those drapes look drab," she points out. It's a never-ending cycle of paint samples, pieces of fabric, tile, wood, carpet samples, different pillows, different lamps, different shades, different furniture, different everything. I start to really like some of her ideas, but by the time I find myself fond of something, she changes it. I'm surprised she hasn't changed me or traded me in for something new and different from Europe. What if I did that with a new vehicle every week? I wonder how excited she would be about that? (But guess what? This isn't about me—it's all about her.)

How about when you're both watching TV, and you flip on a channel that's airing the entire *Rocky* series? All five movies are showing the entire day, commercial-free and back-to-back. You're excited, but she's not. What's the first thing she says? "Please change it. I want to watch *Decorating Disasters with Divas of Design*." That's how easy it is for her to change something that she doesn't like. It might have been the same way when you guys got married. You may have changed somewhere along the way, and now you're different. Changing a channel is nothing compared to changing a lifestyle or changing a bad habit.

That's what this chapter is all about. It's getting back to the person you once were in your relationship with your wife. It could have been before marriage, before kids, after kids, or two weeks ago. It could have been your appearance, your manners, your style, your ideas, or even your attitude. This list isn't going to turn you into a girly man. They're just things that your wife may need you to do more often or less often, depending on the topic. If these ideas relate to you and shed some light on the possibility that you might be able to change a little, then we're headed in the right direction. If they're not for you, that's okay. Just know that *change* is not a dirty word.

It's all about her idea #16: Watch your manners

Why do we feel as men, we can do stuff in front of our wives like burp the alphabet, relieve ourselves of flatulence, and pick our noses, but would never do so in front of our friends, coworkers, our bosses, our children's teachers, and our ministers? The bigger question is, would we have done it the day of our wedding or even while we were dating? Probably not, so why do we do it now, years later, or think that it's okay to do it now? I guess that's why women love using the phrase, "Men act just like animals." It's true; we do. Combine that with licking your fingers after eating, not saying "thank you" after you have received something, not covering your mouth when you sneeze or cough, and chewing your fingernails, and you have yourself a modern-day caveman. Just a guess, but she probably doesn't like the spitting in public or the ice-chewing either.

It's all about her idea #17: Pull out her chair

Not so she can fall down on her rump, but just because it's the gentlemanly thing to do. It's old-fashioned and very old school, but it still works wonders in making your wife feel important. She'll think she's at the White House. If you haven't done it up to this point, that's okay. She'll be surprised, but in a good way. When you go to a restaurant, make sure the waiter or host doesn't do it. That'll certainly kill the moment she wasn't expecting in the first place. In addition to pulling her chair out, stand when she leaves the table. (For bonus points, stand when she returns to the table too.) It's a sign of respect and gives her attention when she leaves the room, and that's where it deserves to be—on her. Don't worry about anyone else looking at you or wondering what you're doing. If women are looking at you while you're doing it, they're probably thinking, "Oh, what a sweet gesture. I wish my husband would do that." If men are wondering what you're doing, they're probably thinking you have ants in your pants or you're having underwear issues, unless, of course, they treat their wives with the same respect. Then they'll just smile at you in recognition that you've also had some training.

It's all about her idea #18: Open the door

It doesn't matter if it's a car door or a front door, as a gentleman you should always do this for anyone, but most importantly for your wife. Granted, she's not the Queen of England, but this will certainly make her feel that she is the queen of your heart. It's a kind gesture, and whether she admits it or not, she likes it.

When you do, make sure you pull it open first, allow her to walk in with you following, not the other way around. Prove to her that chivalry is not dead.

It's all about her idea #19: Have her choose your clothes

This one is tough because you're most likely thinking what I thought when my wife did this for me the very first time: "Oh, great, she's either going to make me look really retro like one of those metrosexual types or really frumpy and weird so my friends make fun of me." Well, she didn't, and they didn't, either. She actually knew what she was doing and bought clothes that fit my style. The caveat to this is to make sure she is knowledgeable about style and not more hapless than you. She should know better, but you never know. You don't want to look at your outfit afterward and say, "This isn't going to work. There's too much metro and not enough hetero." Most women purchase their husband's "outfits" anyway, so why not let her instruct you on how to wear them? You can't tell the difference between winter clothes and spring clothes, so why do you care? You wear sandals before Easter and often after Labor Day.

It's all about her idea #20: Clean your side of the closet

Sure, your wife doesn't mind breaking her ankle every time she has to go to your side of the closet. For many women, this "trek to the other side" is like climbing a mountain. Pick up the pile of clothes, move the shoes, hang up the hangers, and throw away the plastic garment bags and tags that come from the cleaners. Clear the pathway so she won't have to beg you to do it. If you take your clothes to the cleaners, ask for a cleaning bag. Most cleaners give these out. Put the cleaning bag in the closet and refill it every time you think about throwing your clothes on the ground. When it gets full, take it in. When you go out on the town wearing a newly starched shirt, she won't have people staring at the bruises on her ankles.

It's all about her idea #21: Have that exam she's wanted you to have

Who doesn't love it when doctors take their fingers and jam them up rear ends for a rectal exam? It's not like you have to take the doctor out afterwards on a date. Compared to what women have to go through, we should be happy. Plus, I'm sure the doctor isn't too thrilled looking at your backside either. We've probably all seen the movie *Fletch*, where Chevy Chase gets a rectal exam and reacts to it with a song of astonishment. It's not known whether Chase's character was over forty, but it is recommended that men over that age have a yearly rectal exam to check the prostate gland. A colonoscopy is also something you may need to have done. It's nowhere near as bad as it sounds, and it might save your life. Your wife wants to keep you around a while. She's not ready for you to go just yet, so either do this or continue listening to the nagging. She's also sick of you complaining about the toothache you've had for six months now. Get it checked out.

It's all about her idea #22: Put the seat down

I've actually timed this. It takes less than two seconds to take your hand, grab the lid, and pull down. It takes zero effort and requires no energy at all; it's actually trapping and keeping foul smells from entering the ozone, but we still can't seem to grasp the concept of shutting the dumb thing.

First of all, which one is she talking about? Is she talking about the seat part or the actual lid? That's what I'm always confused about. The seat refers to what you sit on. I'll have that down already, take care of business, flush, leave the room, and still hear, "Put the seat down next time!" *What? I just did. The seat is down. Is she talking about the lid?* That's what confuses most men. We're not sure which one should be down all the time. From now on, just do both, and she won't ever bug you about this again.

It's all about her idea #23: Flush the toilet

It's not like your wife doesn't enjoy looking at your waste product, but this goes hand in hand with idea #22. If you don't do either, then you just need to go to etiquette school right now. If you share a toilet and you accidentally miss (you know what I'm talking about), for the love of decency, clean it up. Your wife doesn't need any more surprises.

It's all about her idea #24: Replace the used roll

This is your own home, for crying out loud, meaning that's exactly what your wife does every time you use the last square and don't replace it—she cries. First of all, you're not six, and even a six-year-old would know to at least inform his mommy that the roll is empty. If you're out, go buy some more, or at least let someone else know before they use the restroom. It's very frustrating to know that they'll be helpless because you were thoughtless.

It's all about her idea #25: Hang up the towel

You're not the swamp monster from the black lagoon. You had a little dirt but washed it off. You're dry now, so why not hang your towel up and use it again? Remember, every time a towel gets thrown on the floor or put in the hamper, your wife has to wash it again. That gets you two things: 1.) You just wasted some of the time she has to spend with you, and 2.) You have less money at the end of the month because of your high water bill. That means she's lost some time, and you can't afford to take her out and show her off. Wipe your wet feet on the mat and quit dropping the towel to use as a bath mat. Hang it up, let it dry, use it again. If you need a mat, any Target, Walmart, K-Mart, or Walgreens has them for less than ten dollars.

It's all about her idea #26: Use a glass

I admit I still drink out of the carton—but only because I drink skim milk and the rest of my family drinks two-percent. So maybe that's what you ought to do. Whether it's milk, orange juice, soda, or tea, there's nothing more disgusting than seeing a grown man drink out of a carton and then put it back into the refrigerator. You just robbed the rest of your family from experiencing the joy of that beverage by not using a glass. Not only that, you also just set back the progression of men thousands of years. What's worse is that you probably do it all the time and don't tell anyone. Shame on you and your germ-infested mouth. What if your wife went out to your car and mixed water with your oil? She would ruin your car. That's exactly what you just did.

It's along the same lines as dipping a chip after it's been in your mouth. It's gross and disgusting, and you should be flogged with the chips. While you're in the kitchen, she also probably doesn't like it when you forget to put the twist-tie back on the bread. She knows you're the one who's been doing that. You can't spin the bag around and stick the loaf back in the cupboard. It doesn't work. It squeezes the top piece and ruins the rest of the loaf. Be sure to close the cereal box properly, too. Apparently, we're supposed to roll down the plastic bag inside and slide the small tab into the slot on the big tab.

It's all about her idea #27: Soften the tone

Stressed out or not, your wife is always looking for a calm, rational, level-headed partner who doesn't blow up at every little thing. You both work. You both deal with the same stress, fear, and anxiety everyone else does: kids, money, bills, insurance, and sickness. Why not solve the world's problems together and not carry the burden on your own? Keep things together when it seems like they're falling apart. Not only is your wife depending on it, but your boss, coworkers, family, and kids are also. When a problem does come up, keep things on the cool side and not the dark side.

It's all about her idea #28: Help her make the bed

You're absolutely right; it doesn't make sense why there are seventeen pillows on your bed and no one ever sees your room, but it's something women love to do. This is just a simple way to make her day easier. Whether she works at home or works at an office, it takes five minutes with your help. The bottom sheet that's covering the mattress will probably stay on. It just depends on how dirty you are. So you may actually start with the top sheet. It goes under the top blanket or comforter, whichever one you guys use. You spread that out nice and flat, then the top blanket goes on top, then the comforter. After you stuff the edges of bottom sheet and top blanket between the mattress and dust ruffle, you'll then fold the comforter back, stick the sleeping pillows on top of the sheets, and then unfold the comforter back on to the pillows toward the wall. Then straighten out the sheets and get all the wrinkles out. After that, you'll probably have "accessory pillows" to place on top of the comforter. It's a bigger deal than you think. It'll take her half the time if you assist her. (If you're late to work because you stayed and helped, I don't recommend telling your coworkers the exact reason you are late. Of course, if you do, tell them you got the idea out of a highly recommended, hysterical book titled *150 Secrets to a Happy Wife* by Joe Gumm.)

It's all about her idea #29: Walk with her, not in front of her

Are we in that much of a hurry? Is there a race going on somewhere that we're trying to win? Does your wife smell that badly that you have to walk in front of her? This happens a lot more often than you'll notice, especially with couples that have been married for a while. You'll find that the man always walks in front of the woman. It doesn't matter if it's at the mall, in a parking lot, at the beach, at a concert, or at the park, it always happens. Couples who are dating are inseparable. As the years go by, they stop holding hands, but they're still walking side by side. Many years later, the man starts slowly edging his way forward, as if he's not interested in walking beside his wife anymore. Then you'll notice, as the couple gets really old, they'll start walking together again. Usually that's because the man needs help staying upright. While you're at it, hold hands, too. Act like you've been in love for the last ten, fifteen, twenty years. Holding hands never gets boring, and it shows everyone that you're a couple. Show her you're still in love with her.

It's all about her idea #30: Don't mock her when she's trying to be serious

How many times have we done this before? The argument starts, it gets heated, she says something that gets you going, and all of a sudden, the high-pitched jeering begins. It's just like goading a donkey or a horse. You're trying to get your wife all riled up. This is what usually puts my wife over the edge. I start making fun of her during an argument and stoop to the junior high level. It's a mechanism that automatically kicks in. It's stupid, immature, and just dumb. I don't accomplish one thing in doing it. She usually gets offended, the argument stops, and nothing is accomplished. I usually end up apologizing for the argument and acting the way I did.

To be quite honest, I really think she gets offended not because of what I'm doing, but because when I'm mocking her, I'm not even close to sounding like her. I do this really horrible southern drawl with a redneck twang. She doesn't sound like that at all. I know it's very infantile, and I also know she's smarter than me when it comes to being serious. I revert to elementary-school tactics; she doesn't. If it's this way with you, try doing your impressions for something other than mocking your wife. Try working with puppets, and become a ventriloquist.

Chapter Five

How to Marry out of Your League

"I married beneath me. All women do."

—Lady Nancy Astor, English politician and first female
member of the British Parliament

I lied to my wife! I can finally admit it.

I've been holding that in since I married her in May of 1997.
I actually wanted to admit it to her privately in a conversation at
her favorite jewelry store, but I think the way I've done it (in the
fifth chapter of a very popular book that millions of women will
read) was the way to go.

Actually, my lie came in the form of false advertising. I pre-
sented it to her in a physical package, sort of the way companies
advertise their products on TV. We've all seen the commercial
that shows the delicious, mouth-watering hamburger with all
the toppings piled high. You get to the restaurant and plop down
almost four dollars for what looks like a smashed Frisbee. There
are no flames burning in the background, no free-wheeling chefs
slicing and dicing vegetables, and you most certainly don't need
two hands to pick it up and eat it.

It's called great marketing. It's a way for companies to get
by with presenting something that's not one hundred percent

accurate, instead of coming out and saying, "We're lying to you about this product." In my case, I lied about my product: my body. My wife thought I was just about perfect physically because that's what I made it look like—with my clothes on. When we eventually got married, it didn't take her too long to realize that not only did my feet stink (even after a shower), but the hair on my head was receding, I had back fur that needed to be shaved once a month, my toes turned inward, my nose hair was somewhat out of control for being in my early twenties, and I had a unibrow that grew faster than my beard. All of a sudden, I'm the smashed Frisbee.

Of course, that's how a lot of men market their product, every day, all the time, 24/7, morning, noon, and night, 365 days a year. We use false advertising to win over our girlfriends, they become our fiancées, and we eventually marry them. Good for us, bad for women.

The question now isn't, "Why do men do this?" The question is, "Why do women fall for it?" We know, as men, we have nothing else. We realize women are superior at everything. We tell stupid jokes, play with bubble wrap for hours, recite lines from movies we've seen a hundred times, and chase squirrels with weed whackers. Even still, with a flawed package, women end up paying the four dollars for a flat burger and end up marrying someone they may regret marrying down the line.

I wasn't trying to hide my physical abnormalities when I got married, but I also wasn't going to embarrass my wife in front of God and about five hundred guests by saying something like, "Will you, Alexa, take me, Joe, a very pasty-colored, very sub-par physical specimen to be your furry love machine for the next sixty years?" either.

Believe me, I would've loved to have gotten electrolysis before we got married, but I found out that spending five minutes every third Thursday of the month with my wife shaving my back is a lot cheaper, and it's the bonding time we've really come to appreciate. Plus, when I'm sixty-three, we'll have enough hair for a collection of throw pillows.

To this day, I'm still surprised she agreed to go out with me on a first date, then, unbelievably, a second one. Of course, it didn't take too long for me to realize two things: 1.) that she was young and naïve, and 2.) that I needed to act on that before it was too late and she realized she had made a terrible mistake. That point was made evident years later after we, as husband and wife, went to a company Christmas party. The next day at work, my colleagues crowned me president of the "I married way out of my league" club. I wasn't offended, because from day one I always knew I would act, look, sound, smell, feel, and speak better because of my wife. It was the old adage, "Behind every successful man, there's a woman." Or in my case, "Behind every successful man, there's a woman—pushing." It was true for us: the ultimate "from the other side of the tracks" story. She captivated me with her smile, grace, love, and beauty. I captured her with my comedy, my self-deprecation, my roofing job, the remedial courses I was taking at a community college, the 1978 Ford F-150 I had bought for $300, and my very large and very noticeable Adam's apple.

Though I still had several rough edges that needed to be smoothed, she was just about flawless. That meant I had some major catching up to do. I knew that if I wanted to keep her, I needed to do several things, including stop eating like it was my last meal. I would hover over my food and shovel it down my throat like I was in a race. I now know why I had heartburn all the time. She put up with the hover/shovel method of eating, but barely. She gave me some leeway. I learned to sit up and actually bring the fork up to my mouth and eat more slowly—like other humans. I was also able to breathe a lot better. That was an easy one. The scruffy beard look wasn't.

I never liked shaving and always thought it was cool to have a little peach fuzz on my face. It seemed like that was always the sign of a masculine man—how much hair he had on his face or body. I remember a time in eighth grade when I was changing for a basketball game and I took off my shirt. I looked like a large sphinx cat: nice and smooth. I had nothing on my face and certainly nothing under my arms or on my chest. My friend Michael was a different story. When he took his shirt off, every other hairless chin in that locker room dropped to the floor. No one on the team could believe how hairy he was. He was a man among boys. He was hairier than most of our dads. He had a five o'clock shadow, that's how old he looked. We all started asking each other what that was. We had never seen that much fur on a kid our age. Me? I was just puny and pathetic. Not only did I put my jersey on with lightning speed, I put an undershirt on under it. If I had a turtleneck handy, I would've used that. We all would have, except Michael.

Years later, I finally grew patches on my face and wanted to show off the little amount I had. That type of thinking didn't go over too well when it was time to kiss the girl of my dreams. It seemed like every time we kissed, she would go away with razor burn. She never really said anything, but I finally figured it out. I wasn't making her flush with passion; I was slowly ripping the flesh off her face. Needless to say, I started shaving before dates. It was that simple.

So the shaving and the eating, my future wife could handle. The combat boots and holes in the jeans she couldn't. That's when I did an about-face and turned everything over to her from that point on. Out with the old, and in with the new. I didn't do it because she told me to do it. I did it because I realized she knew better than I did. She wanted me to change for the better. It wasn't a selfish move on her part. I was smart enough to know that patches of hair on my face, holes in my clothes, and clod hoppers on my feet weren't going to get me a better-paying job or move me up the ladder any faster at work. She also knew the ins and outs of fashion and knew what clothes of mine needed to be discarded. Mine were so pathetic, that sadly, even Goodwill wouldn't take them. I became a better person for it. I also became naked. I had nothing left. She threw it all out.

Although I'm only 90 percent free of the rough edges, I'm still a work-in-progress, but I work hard at trying to attain 100 percent status (something that may or may not happen in her lifetime). For most women, it's different. They're always trying to improve on how they look, dress, smell, feel, and sound, and they work hard at making the effort. They're relentless. It doesn't matter if it's for a date, church, school, a restaurant, carpool, a baseball game, or just sitting around the house in pajamas. They're always trying to look their best. A mirrored and lighted compact is never far away. Plus, they want us to look our best, because they're allowing us to escort and be seen with them in public. We should appreciate that. Either that, or we should buy them expensive gifts.

Just take a look inside a woman's medicine cabinet, and try to figure out what is in there and what all of the products do. You can't do it. There's no possible way you could tell me what Visible Skin Renewer is and its purpose. What about hygiene products? You want to know how many of these things women have around the house? I say around the house, because that's how much space they need to store it all. It's infinite. Once you think you have a grasp on how much there is, that's when you discover another drawer or cabinet or basket full of stuff. Now take a guess how many hygiene products men need? Not have, just need. One. One, that's it. It's deodorant. If we smell like body odor around women, they won't like us very much. Those of you who guessed toothpaste were close, but look at it this way: if you're wearing strong enough deodorant, she won't smell your bad breath. Plus, no amount of toothpaste will ever cover up B.O. We know what to do with our one product, and we think using more products like cologne, hairspray, and mouthwash will help. We just need to listen to our wives when it comes to how to use them appropriately.

Women are high maintenance because they have to be. It's not their job; it's their birthright. We enjoy it because they actually look good as finished products. How much effort do they put into it? Try waxing your legs. What about putting on a pair of pantyhose? This is called "work" to men. To women, it's a necessity. They wear

underwire undergarments, paint fingernails and toenails, exfoli-
ate, and wax certain body parts that are way too close for comfort
(men would never do this more than once), pluck their eyebrows,
get facials, moisturize, wear thong underwear, shave more body
parts than we do, and still understand what a two-year-old child
says, word for word. Too good to be true? Maybe. The more domi-
nant species on planet Earth? Absolutely yes!

We watch wrestling, lick our fingers, smack while eating,
wear clothes that don't match, adjust our private areas in front of
thousands of people on the baseball field and on live TV, and we
can't do two things at once. We have more hair in our noses and
ears than we do on the top of our heads. We growl like dogs and
bump chests when we greet each other (women can't physically
do that). We sweat; they perspire. We zip up and go, and they
have straps, buttons, clips, zippers, ties, and buckles. Their lives
are much more complicated than ours, but they have a better
chance of looking better as they get older. Men? We start off as
babies looking like everyone else, but the chances of ending up
looking like the fourth man on the evolutionary chart is possible. This is especially true if women aren't around.

Even if they are around and they make us look better than what
we once looked like, I know there will still be women who see us
with our wives and think, "How in the world did he get her? I
bet he has tons of money." Guys are no different. They're thinking
the same thing: "Boy, he sure did out-kick his coverage." That's
okay, though. We're not changing our looks for other people. We're
changing our looks for our wives. If she's happy about what she
sees when she wakes up in the morning, then that's all that matters.

So, if you're a diamond in the rough, a rough diamond, or even a cubic zirconium, this chapter gives you fifteen ideas on how to never revert to those old ways and how to continue with the project until completion. Sometimes it's not so easy and may take longer than expected. If you already do these things and you're just about perfect, read them anyway. You may want to suggest them to someone who is still under renovation (like a buddy).

It's all about her idea #31: Take out the garbage

Unless you like the smell of maggots in your pantry, make sure this is done on a regular basis. Don't just go by and push the load down, as if it appears less full than it is. Your wife is smarter than that. Do it when it's filled up and not when it's been sitting in the kitchen for days smelling like dirty diapers, old fish, bad fruit, coffee grounds, or onions. There's nothing worse than having a beautiful kitchen and a foul odor lurking in the shadows. Do it because it's your job, and always make sure she doesn't have to. Don't forget to check the garbage cans in the other rooms. (Men always seem to forget that.)

It's all about her idea #32: Don't put your clothes on the ground—all the time

Especially if you work at an oil-changing facility or you're a coal miner. Now, yes, it would be nice if we could walk around our house like Adam walked around the Garden of Eden.

Unfortunately, we can't be naked all the time. We have to wear clothes, and sometimes they end up on the floor of the closet. Living with four little girls, I understand why my wife hates this. My girls do exactly what every other female on the planet does— try on something, throw it on the ground, and try five more pieces on. Okay, so maybe men don't do it that much, but it's still a pain for your wife to have to lean down, pick it up, hang it up, or wash it, when it could have easily been done the first time.

Maybe it should never have been thrown on the floor. It just depends on how patient your wife is. If she's like my wife, she never wants them on the ground. She'll just step right over them. Serves you right. You're not in college anymore, and guess who gets to pick them up every time you do it? Your wife does. All of that bending over has taken a toll on her. Plus, she's told you to either hang them up or put them in the hamper or the bag that's going to the cleaners. If you have smaller kids, they may end up doing the same thing you do. You spent money on those clothes, and if you have kids, it's not like you can buy new ones every month. (Clothes, not kids.) Reduce the wear and tear and keep them off the floor. (Clothes, not kids.)

It's all about her idea #33: Try to use proper grammar

Don't get me wrong, your wife loves the fact that your eight-year-old speaks better than you—it's endearing. However, this is a tough one, because so many men are set in their ways when it comes to using the right word while trying to form a sentence that makes sense. If you're like me, you didn't learn anything in high school English because you really didn't care for it. College wasn't any easier, but you passed. So now you're in the real world and interviewing with a Fortune 500 company. You have to go through six interviews, but you didn't pass the first one because you used "should've went" instead of "should've gone," or "was" instead of "were," or "I've already ate" instead of "I've already eaten," or said something else you shouldn't have. The way you dressed may have impressed the interviewer, but maybe your English didn't. One little miscue, and you missed out on a jackpot of a job. Why? Because you don't speak correctly. Either go enroll in a community college or listen to your wife. She actually paid attention in English class and earned an A. Swallow your pride and pay attention to what she's telling you to say. You may learn something that'll give you a verbal advantage for the next job interview.

It's all about her idea #34: Read

A magazine, a book, a newspaper, even a bathroom stall…pick something to read. If you've ever had a conversation with your wife where she says she bought you a book and you replied, "I saw the movie. I don't need to read the book," then you probably need to read more books. Don't pull the old "I did the CliffsNotes" thing either. I did the CliffsNotes thing and didn't retain any of it.

We were walking in a mall, and my wife said something like, "Oh, that painting over there on the wall, next to the Gap, looks like a Mondrian." I replied, "What's a Mondrian?" She then went into this lengthy diatribe about how Piet Mondrian was a famous painter of landscapes but then became very popular with his abstract style, mostly because of his influence in Cubism. I then asked, "How did you know that?" Simply, she said, "I read." Talk about putting me in my place. I didn't know about a painter from the early twentieth century who left Europe during World War II and came to the United States; she got me on that one.

Of course, as soon as she made the "I read" comment, I asked her if she knew who the last person in the majors was to hit .400. She didn't know. She also couldn't tell me if forty-five thousand people ever showed up to see the works of Mondrian at one sitting, like they do for a pennant race in baseball.

Hey, from day one, I've always admitted that my wife has the book smarts and I have the street smarts. She has the book smarts because she's been reading since age five. I, on the other hand, can spurt out movie quotes on demand. That's how I know I need to read more. Not just newspapers and magazines, and not just books with pictures—real ones that have words. Evidently, books about dead painters, too. Maybe you do, too. You don't ever want your child to have to explain to you the reason why the sky is blue. He'll either know it because he read it somewhere or Mommy told him. Believe it or not, it's not because "it was painted that way."

It's all about her idea #35: Stop eating or drinking the one thing she doesn't like

"You know that's not good for you, don't you?" "That's going to kill you." Hate hearing that all the time? Me too. This one is tough for most men because you know as well as I do that men have a hard time stopping something once they get started. For some men, it is beer or ice cream. It's diet cola for me; it could be pizza, donuts, chips, or coffee for you. Whatever "it" is, major damage is being done to your belly, cholesterol, heart, lungs, whatever. Your wife wants you to be around to see the kids graduate, get married, and have kids of their own. Live a while, won't you? Just say no, or in this case, "No, thank you." Replace that one thing with rice patties, tofu, cauliflower, bean sprouts, or something that's really low in fat—dirt.

It's all about her idea #36: Take her to a concert, opera, theater, or museum— something that is cultural

In other words, take her to something you really don't like that's cultured. Sure, putt-putt golf is exciting, and even dinner and a movie are nice, but every time you go out together? Why not impress her with something different, something that sparks interest from your wife, not just you? Sure, she would probably never complain about the same shoot-em-up, action hero movie you see at the cinema-plex, but how about expanding your horizons? If you've never watched a fat man belt out high octaves, an opera is something to see. Try even going to a concert that *she* likes. What about ballet with men in tights running around on their tippy toes? You may not enjoy it, but she'll enjoy the costumes and pageantry. How about a museum? You never know; you may get inspired to be her little Picasso. She may be tired of the same flick and burger joint, so think outside the box on this one (not the burger box).

It's all about her idea #37: Show emotion

Which really means we all want you to cry. How does your wife know she can talk to you about anything if she never gets anything back? Emotion can be a look, a sound, a noise, laughing, crying, whatever. Don't ever be afraid of a tender or touching moment. Express yourself with emotions. Show something to let her know what you're thinking and that you're not dead inside. Don't suppress emotion and then one day have a huge explosion. Don't keep her guessing, either.

Yes, women do have ESP, and they know a lot more than we think they know, but when it comes to having a special moment of togetherness, don't shy away from it. There may be people at work you share everything with, a laugh, a smile, a joke, a funny story. Don't be more connected to them than you are with your wife. She's supposed to be your best friend.

It's all about her idea #38: Quit using all the hot water in the shower

This idea was actually submitted to me by a woman living in Antarctica. Okay, it was actually submitted by my wife. "You're not on *American Idol*, so quit singing," she said to me years ago, after I steamed up the bathroom with a thirty-seven-minute shower. It's not like your wife doesn't enjoy the medley of falsetto '80s rock songs you sing in the shower, but let her go first, especially if it's in the morning and you're both rushed. This isn't a stage, and you're not performing. Men should not be spending twenty or thirty minutes in the shower. It's mostly used to wake you up in the morning, anyway, not as a sauna. Wash the hair, brush the teeth, shave, clean off, and let your wife enjoy all the hot water. Either that, or shower at night or in another bathroom. The extra time you don't spend in the shower you can spend primping in front of the mirror. (Something you probably need to do more of anyway.) You want your wife to get the hot water first, so when you get in, the ice-cold water can hit your flesh like a fly hits a moving windshield.

It's all about her idea #39: Slow down

Correct me if I'm wrong, but wasn't the movie *The Fast and the Furious* taken from this scenario? You drive fast, get a ticket, and your wife gets furious. Actually, the reason your wife doesn't like you driving 85 in a 60 mph zone is because she loves you and wants to keep you around for a while. (Plus, speeding tickets are a waste of money.) Slow things down, Evil Knievel. Go to a place that has go-carts or simulated cars. You can usually find plenty of racing there. Take the kids, or take some buddies. Get it all out of your system there—not on the highway. If you're driving fast with your kids in the car, your license should be revoked. You can still jam the music; just cool the speedometer, Speed Racer. If you have kids, you're probably jamming out to cartoon songs, rap music, or the latest boy bands anyway. Just remember something a little old lady told me years ago: "The angels leave your car after you go past the speed limit." Something to think about.

It's all about her idea #40: Take her advice

Whether it's wearing a different shirt, applying for a new job, treating family members differently, or combing your hair in a different style, always take her advice. Not sometimes, not most of the time, not once a month or a couple of days a week—always. For some reason, women seem to know how things are going to turn out. Call it intuition, ESP, God—maybe all of the above.

Whatever it is, women seem to have more of a level head when it comes to playing psychic. They know more about pop culture and what goes on in this world than we do. If you don't like taking her advice and you think the guys at work will make fun of the pink shirt you're wearing (it's not salmon; it's pink), agree to disagree, but find a middle ground. If something she tells you turns out to be right, I guarantee she probably won't gloat about it. That's usually what we do when we give advice to our wives about "guy stuff," and it turns out that we were right (which is rare).

It's all about her idea #41: Have a maid come in

Don't wait for your wife's birthday or anniversary or anything special. Do this when she's not expecting it. Do it on a day when her list of things to do is a mile long. Do it when the kids are out of the house for school. Do it when her stress level has reached the intolerable level. Do it when the shadows under her eyes are a heavy charcoal. Do it when she needs to get some rest. Do it before she breaks down and cries. Have a whole team come in and brighten her day just by cleaning her world. Believe me, you'll be able to punch your "Husband of the Year" ticket with this one. Of course, you're not doing it for that reason anyway, but no doubt, hugs and kisses will follow.

It's all about her idea #42: She controls the remote from now on

Did you ever hear the story about the man that gave up all control of his remote to please his wife? No? I didn't either, because you still have control of it. I agree, *The Simpsons* are still TV gold after over twenty years of being on the air, but for crying out loud, detach the thing from your hand and give it up once in a while. What do think that means, *remote control?* It means you have too much control of the remote. Do it for an hour, a night, a weekend, or a month.

Believe it or not, couples get in huge arguments over the remote. It happens all the time, or at least with my parents. For some reason, my dad thinks since he bought the remote for nine bucks at Radio Shack, it's his and his alone. I think I've actually heard him tell my mom, "Go get your own." These days, there are tons of things you can do to watch what you want and still give up the control of the remote. There's TiVo; there's picture in picture; you can even record your program in the other room. There are plenty of things to argue about; this should not be one of them. If it ever gets to that, just give up the dumb thing and let her watch what she wants. If you don't like watching baby stories, cooking shows, or soap operas, go read a book. (How about one about that famous painter?)

It's all about her idea #43: Don't drink and smoke for at least a day

I don't do either, but I know a lot of people who do. If these are some of your vices, why not give them up for at least a day? It's not as if she's asking you to give them up forever. Maybe she is, but a day would be a lot nicer than never stopping. Come home from work and grab a cola instead of a beer and spend that five minutes of smoke time playing with your kids instead. Your wife has had a stressful day, too, but she doesn't have to depend on cigs and beer to relax. Who knows? Maybe by not doing it for a day, you'll begin the first stage of breaking the habit (if it is a habit). If it's not a habit and she wants you to stop completely, why not do it? Why continue to have the same discussion over and over again? If your house smells like a chimney or your fridge has more alcohol in it than food, maybe those are signs that you're spending way too much money and way too much time on them both. Plus, you have the accompanying health issues, too. Try it for a day and see what happens.

It's all about her idea #44: Don't go to bed mad

Obviously, this only means if you get in an argument or fight. Yes, I had to actually explain this to a woman at a conference, who wanted me to understand that she and her husband never argued or fought. For those of you that aren't perfect and do this, it's never a good thing. First of all, arguing for men is theatrical. It's a sport. There are a lot of things we're not good at, but arguing is something we can do all night long. We act stuff out, we use props, use lifelines, phone friends, and get help from the audience. It's a talent. It's a gift. We bring stuff up from the past, the present, and the future, and even make stuff up. We shouldn't do it, but sometimes it happens, and we regret it. Come to a truce, agree to disagree, apologize, so that everyone can hit the sack in time to get some sleep. Either that, or keep it going all night long and be zombies the next day. Of course, I'm not saying put the argument on hold and continue it the next day just so you can get in your eight hours. I'm saying that if you argue, and it's around bedtime, it's probably a good idea to make sure everything is resolved before your heads touch the pillows.

It's all about her idea #45: Quit messing around on the computer

What is so important on the World Wide Web that you can't spend time at work figuring it out? It's just another object that takes time away from your children or your wife. Now, obviously, if you're using it for educational purposes or doing stuff like planning a vacation, paying bills, or looking up times for movies, it's definitely a necessity. If you're busy reading the Facebook statuses of your 2,854 friends (2,534 of whom you really don't know), playing Doom or Solitaire, or checking your fantasy football team, you need to have your fingers cut off. No wonder your wife's mad at you before you go to bed.

Chapter Six

How to Talk with One Foot in Your Mouth

"A study in the Washington Post *says that women have better verbal skills than men. I just want to say to the authors of that study: 'Duh!'"*

—Conan O'Brien, late night talk show host and comedian

Have you ever tried to walk with one foot stuck in your mouth? If you're a man or a circus performer who travels the country, you've done this before. "Think before you speak." We're told to do this all the time. Somehow, we tend to forget this any time we're around a group of people, and we unintentionally blurt out something to embarrass our wives. When it comes to saying dumb things, men are the absolute best at doing this. It doesn't matter if it's at church when the offering plate is being passed: "Honey, do you think the pastor will mind if I get change for a dollar when the offering plate comes by? I'd like to get a soda after church." Or when we're at the hospital looking at our friends' baby for the first time in the nursery: "Are you sure he's yours? He doesn't look a bit like you or your wife. He does resemble your accountant though." We say dumb things. We know that. That's easy for us. Trying to stop saying dumb things, especially to our wives, is hard. That's why you have to know what's dumb and what's not dumb.

When you tell your wife something like, "Do you think you can do something about your halitosis next time we kiss? A breath mint, gum, something, please. My gosh, it's like making out with the trash can," that's dumb. Saying something like, "You smell good. What is that you're wearing, Pledge?" that's not necessarily dumb, because you did compliment her when you said she smelled good. But then it's not necessarily good, because you said she smelled like a cleaning product. I say stuff that's in my subconscious mind all the time that I know I shouldn't be held responsible for. My wife gives me some leeway on that. Those things, I think, are forgivable. They're in your subconscious mind. You're not responsible for that. When you're at a restaurant and your wife orders a dessert and you say, "Are you really going to eat that?" meaning you probably thought she was full from her dinner, that's a very good question and shows concern about her health on your part. However, she probably heard it like this: "I can't believe you're actually going to eat dessert, you big, fat chunk of lard grease. After what you already ate tonight, you're really going to indulge in something that's going to add more fat on your already large frame? You should be ashamed of yourself, you fat sack of fat." That's how she heard it.

Saying things you're knowingly responsible for, those are the things we have to watch. Those are the things you say to your wife, and then after you say them, you go, "Oh, geez. I can't believe I just said that," or "Shoot, why did I say that? That was so dumb." You follow that up with a hand-to-the-head slap or something else that signifies a dumb statement. It could be a story, a joke, singing, dancing, on purpose, or by accident. This chapter tells us why we say the things we say and offers the perfect solution to help us permanently put a leash on our tongues.

I remember one particular time my wife took me to a dinner party for her interior design friends. You noticed I said, "took me"? Everything was great. I was acting my best. Charm school was paying off, and the brainwashing was working. However, halfway through the party, things turned ugly. It all started when I had more than my share of Diet Coke. I was on my fifth can and remember mixing in some fudge brownies and ice cream. That much caffeine and sugar can't be good for anyone. That's when my tongue loosened and the saga began.

I found myself bored to tears with her friends talking about drapes and backsplashes and coffered ceilings. If you don't know what those terms mean, don't worry. Ninety-eight percent of men in America don't know either. (In France, ninety-eight percent of men do know.) Anyway, at that point, I decided that they needed a story that would put an end to theirs. I went into an elaborate tale to paint the right picture of my first rectal exam, which I had experienced just weeks before. Now you know what I was talking about when I said it would put an end to their stories.

If I had had flash cards and a flannelgraph, I would have used them. I didn't, so I had to depict the wildest image they could imagine in their own minds. I actually started off the story with a few women listening. Then a crowd of five or six gathered. All of a sudden, there was a group of people surrounding me as if I were the famous architect Mies van der Rohe talking about the Barcelona chair. That's Barcelona, not Barcalounger.

Everyone seemed to be intrigued about how I went into the

doctor's office with an injured shoulder and ended up getting a rectal exam. Everyone seemed intrigued except my wife. Once she realized what story I was telling, she slowly began to get a pained expression on her face and was giving me "the look." She was also trying to figure out how to leave gracefully, without anyone noticing. During the story, I glanced at her for an instant, and she had that "I'm smiling on the outside but crying on the inside" expression. You know the kind, with the over emphasized smile, where your forehead wrinkles up and it looks like you're hurting at the same time. You almost look like the Joker trying to figure out an algebra problem, but also trying not to squint from the sun shining in your face. That was the look she had on her face, but I knew she wasn't really smiling. To me it was as fake as could be. I think she was holding back anger or tears.

I wrapped up the story, and we eventually left. I went away from the party with a whole new group of friends. They thought I was a complete weirdo and felt sorry for my wife, but they thought my story was amusing. My reserved wife went away red faced and terribly horrified at the spectacle I had made. My enjoyment of the night combined with her disgust didn't make for good company. I knew I had messed up by telling the story and tried to figure out a way to make it up to her. From that point on, I promised I would consult her and get her approval before telling questionable stories. Forging that solution not only helped our relationship, but it also helped her keep her interior designer friends.

That's why this next list is so important. Whether good, bad, or ugly, the words that come out of your mouth are vital to your wife and kids. No one ever keeps score of the hurtful things that are said when my wife and I argue, but I always know my words are harsher than hers. I can be cruel and sadistic all in the same sentence. But there are also times when we're not arguing that I can be sweet and nice. That happens a lot more often. That's why the following list includes words and phrases that might need to be said more often, and words and phrases that should be banished forever.

It's all about her idea #46: Quit using terms like *fat, chunky, obese, lard, plump, hefty*

As if you didn't already know women have issues with their bodies, you go and use those words? Do you want to die? Seriously? Maybe your wife has added a few pounds since the day you were married, or maybe her body hasn't gone back to the shape it was before you had kids. *Who cares?!* She's still your wife, and she still loves you just the way you are, even if you look like Shrek. You're adding insult to injury, and you're literally squashing her self-esteem to absolutely nothing. Your wife may already know she has a weight problem and may be dealing with it in her own way. She doesn't need the person who is supposed to love her the most to kid her about that. That person would be you. Come to think of it, whether she's overweight, skinny, short, smells bad, or has six toes or an extended forehead, quit using any and all terms that are detrimental to her self-esteem, especially around friends and family members. You're just a Twinkie away from a heart attack yourself. Use tact at all times. *Beanpole*, *shrimp*, *string bean*, and *tall drink of water* may also be offensive.

It's all about her idea #47: Stop comparing her to other women

Your wife is not your mother, your sister, your best friend's wife, your cousin, your next-door neighbor, or any woman at work. So don't compare her with any of those other women, especially during an argument. That's the worst time to do it.

I remember a time when my wife was sick during the first trimester of her second pregnancy and I couldn't get away with saying anything, and that included anything nice. She couldn't eat, sleep, drive, shower, or do anything because she was so nauseated. With the nausea came resentment. I don't know why, and she didn't know why either. It was just a time she didn't want to be messed with. Her parents and I made sure we did everything and anything to make her comfortable at all times.

After about a month of the sickness, I once again had a breakdown in communication. This time around, though, it was worse than the "It's not about you" comment. I made a suggestion that she act a little nicer, because her family and I were there to take care of her, and she should appreciate that a lot more than she did. Then I said, "You know, Julie (her friend that lived in another state) has three kids and just had kidney stones taken out, and she still manages to go on with life. Why can't you?" And once again, I said it in front of her mother.

Not only did my wife want to cry, throw things, bite me, kill me, and destroy me at that moment, but my mother-in-law did too. I got the worst chewing out I had ever received in my entire life. It was well deserved. My father-in-law, who usually sticks up for me, even got in on it. He told me that even though I think things like that, I should never actually say them. He's a third-degree black belt in Tae Kwon Do, so to make it look like he was also offended by my words, he did some sort of UFC/MMA move on me. I can't really remember what it was because I was unconscious for a few minutes. The reason he did it was so that my mother-in-law and wife wouldn't join forces in dismembering my tongue or some other body part. You don't ever, ever, ever compare your wife with anyone else. You married her because she's unique. Make sure she always knows that. If you have trouble remembering that, just consult your father or father-in-law.

It's all about her idea #48: Find a different way to tell her, "I love you"

Mumble it like a baby does; women always think that's cute. This doesn't necessarily mean you should say it in another language, but if you can say "I love you" in French, all the better. It actually means doing it in a way that surprises her. Write it on the mirror with lipstick, say it with roses on the bed, rent a billboard, put notes all over the house for her to discover once she wakes up in the morning, or mow it into the lawn so the entire neighborhood can see it. Or you can do as I do: put a note on the toilet tank. You can guarantee she will see it first thing in the morning.

It's all about her idea #49: Don't ever use the "D" word

No, it's not *death* or your ex-girlfriend *Donna*, but, if you mention one of those words or the real "D" word, *divorce*, you may experience *death*. In America alone, the divorce rate is more than 50 percent, according to the U.S. Census Bureau. Please don't add to the madness. Mentioning divorce is a relationship killer, and if you ever bring it up, she may actually take you up on it. Just because you're having an argument doesn't mean things have to turn ugly with this word. Using it in the heat of battle may cause more damage, so stay away from it. If you need help remembering this one, go rent the movie *War of the Roses*.

It's all about her idea #50: Stop using terms like *old lady*, *ball and chain*, *nag*, *whipped*, and *the wife* or *the boss*

There shouldn't really have to be an explanation for this, but if you're still using these terms, shame on you. Make no mistake, this is a cutdown to your wife. Show me a woman that actually thinks it's funny when a husband uses those terms, and I'll show you a woman who's either faking a laugh or lying. If you have kids, they may pick up on those words and use them out in public. So instead of, "Mommy, may I have a cookie?" it'll be, "Hey, woman, I want a cookie now."

It's all about her idea #51: Tell her she looks pretty

Tell her she looks pretty, even if she looks ugly. Of course, you won't think that or even say it, but you won't have to—she will. That's how women work. We give them a compliment or tell them they look great, and again, they either shrug, sigh, tell us we're lying, or walk away. They do it with their clothes, their hair, and their makeup. I'll tell my wife in the morning how great her hair looks, and by the afternoon, she's cut it all off and added a new color. Doesn't make sense, I know, but that's the way it works.

Maybe you told your wife she looked pretty before you got married and even did it before you had kids. So why not now? She's the same person, but maybe she looks different. Don't ever wait for your wife to ask you if she's pretty. You'll probably give a lukewarm response (not knowing that you did) and send her into a tailspin of depression. Do it every day, once a week, or every other day, just make sure she hears it often. She wants to know that she's still beautiful. When you introduce her to people, be proud that she's your wife. In a world that's proliferated with competition for them, women need to hear this all the time.

It's all about her idea #52: You're not the baby-sitter; you're the father

Quit telling people, "I'm watching the kids today." No, you're not, you're doing your job as their father. Stop acting like it's the biggest hassle to take the kids for a few hours. You should be happy that they even want to hang out with you. When they get older, you may have to bribe them into hanging out with dear old dad. This is your opportunity to do something active or even proactive. Go to the local video store to get a movie, video games, or snacks and cola. Make it a fun night. Go to the mall. Go see a movie in a theater. Go to a skate park, the botanical gardens, a swimming pool, the lake, or the beach. These are the special moments you'll talk about when you get older.

It's all about her idea #53: Never say something different when she tells you, "I love you"

This would include "Ditto," "Thanks," "Appreciate that," "Cool," "That's great, honey," "Awesome," "Okie dokie," "Nice," and "Me too." What does that last one mean, "Me too"? Does that mean you love yourself? She's saying it from the heart and expects something back that's equally affectionate. Guys don't feel like they want to say it all the time, but women do, and they want to hear it back. Remember, it's better to respond than be silent. A silent response may cause her to think you don't love her. Rapid-fire is what we're looking for here. The faster you say, "I love you," after she says it, the better. If it almost sounds like you're stumbling over her because you said it too fast, she'll think you were thinking about it before her. That's what we call a slam-dunk.

It's all about her idea #54: Make her laugh; tell a joke

Have you ever walked by your wife, when she's thinking about something real serious, and just grabbed a handful of her buttocks? I mean just a handful or even a little pinch. It's completely legal. She's your wife, and that's your bottom. You're not in church, your in-laws aren't around, and you're not at a state dinner. She's either going to appreciate it for its comedy relief, or slap the fire out of your face. Either way, the point of this is to not be so serious. Have some fun with your wife. Remember that word, *fun*? Do the things you used to do when you first met. Your wife loved it when you made her laugh. That's all you had when you first met, a sense of humor and potential. That's why she fell in love with you. Tickle the kids, flirt with your wife, be goofy, act ridiculous, and behave at home like you can't at work. Most women will tell you they either had a serious father who never laughed and was all business or a father who was always a jokester. It's okay to combine the two, just make sure she sees both sides. If nothing works, give her a wedgie. She'll either smile or slap you. It works for clowns at a circus and gets huge laughs when senior football players do it to incoming freshmen.

It's all about her idea #55: Never scold, chastise, or yell at her in public

It's never a good idea to be aggressive and loud, and this will only make you feel worse afterward. It doesn't matter where it is; it's sure to cause a scene and embarrass her to boot. If it's around the kids, no doubt they'll feel the same feeling their mom does: utter humiliation. Plus, you'll look like a bully. Bite your tongue, bite your lip, bite the bullet—whatever the object, hold fast and don't blow your top off until you get somewhere private. By the time you are by yourselves, you may have cooled down or even forgotten what you were mad about. That's probably unlikely, because most guys like to remind their wives of how they were wronged. (Women tend to forgive and forget a lot faster.) Women want to be affirmed, not criticized. You probably wouldn't do it to your dog. Why would you do it to your wife? Remember these three "S" words to help: *stop*, *shut up*, and *smile*.

It's all about her idea #56: Don't cuss

Ever hear a four-year-old say the "F" word? How about the "S" word? If your answer is yes, take a big guess where they heard it? *You*, Mr. Potty Mouth! Sure, it's kind of funny to hear (in some sort of weird, dysfunctional way), but it's also wrong for them to do it and wrong for you to do it in front of your kids or your wife. In my line of work, it's a definite no-no. In fact, if you swear on the radio, you'll get fired and face an individual fine of up to $25,000 and a company fine of up to $250,000. I don't do it off or on the air, but some guys I work with do, and they occasionally slip (off the air, not on). Look at it this way, there are plenty of nasty words your kids can learn on TV and probably at school, too, so why do they need to hear it from you? Keep a lid on it or you may hear Junior call your mother-in-law an S.O.B. at Christmas dinner.

It's all about her idea #57: Use a term of endearment

Honey, dear, snookems, buttercup, love muffin, sweet angel, or *peach blossom* will do. Maybe you did it when you first got married, but now it seems silly. Actually, it's cute and playful and shows affection. Maybe you don't do it anymore because you think you're too mature. Maybe you've replaced the cute names with names like *she devil, the antichrist, hell woman,* or *life destroyer.* Those names aren't as sweet, but at least you're trying. Venture back over to the lighter side of things and try the terms of endearment on this list, or make up some new ones.

It's all about her idea #58: Keep a promise

There's nothing worse than being known as a liar, breaking someone's trust, or being undependable, especially if it is with your wife. As men, we say, "I promise," like its no big deal. We probably use it way too often and probably lie more than women do. We're in situations all the time where we're sort of forced to lie. Playing sports is the perfect example. When you pound a team 15-0 in baseball and you actually run-rule them, why is it that you always say, "Good game," afterward? You know it wasn't a good game. They didn't score one run. We learn this when we're young, and it just follows us into adulthood.

Have you ever been in a situation where your wife will ask you to do something and you're not necessarily paying attention to what she's asking you to do? All you hear is, "Do you promise me you'll do that?" You answer, "Yes, I promise." That's when you get in trouble. She could have just asked you to organize your tools or pull weeds, and you said, "Yes, I promise." What about when you're about to go somewhere, and she asks you how much time is left in the game, and you tell her, "Just thirty more seconds"? You know good and well that when you tell your wife there's just thirty seconds left in the NCAA basketball championship and both teams still have three timeouts, that game might not be over for another forty-five minutes.

Most of the time, if women make us a promise, you can just about take their word to the bank. Your wife can't take your promise to the bank because she knows there will be insufficient funds. We don't like it when we know a mechanic is lying through his teeth about our car. We also don't like it when our buddies lie about their scores on the golf course. That's the way our wives feel, too. Be an example to your kids and show them what true honesty is.

It's all about her idea #59: Give her a card and write a poem

I know this chapter is focusing on things that should be said or not said, but this is about words that aren't spoken. Sometimes it's just easier writing words down that may be hard for us to say. Yes, it may be cheesy, but think of the outcome. She may actually be so overcome with joy she'll have a stroke. Of course the joy part is what we're shooting for, not the stroke. Come up with something witty and creative. If you want to, lead in with the "Roses are red" beginning and go from there. She'll get a giggle out of it, and you'll look like a historical romance writer.

It's all about her idea #60: Say thank you every once in a while

Why not? Especially if you accomplish your small list of things that make men happy, you should definitely thank her for that. She does so many things you would never do. We go through nothing compared to our wives. They're just two little words. Use them all the time to show her how much you appreciate her. If you need a reason why, take a look at your kids. That alone should warrant a few "thank you" moments here and there.

Chapter Seven

Lazy Is as Lazy Does

"In the past decade or so, the women's magazines have taken to running home-handyperson articles suggesting that women can learn to fix things just as well as men. These articles are apparently based on the ludicrous assumption that men know how to fix things, when in fact all they know how to do is look at things in a certain squinty-eyed manner, which they learned in Wood Shop; eventually, when enough things in the home are broken, they take a job requiring them to transfer to another home."

—Dave Barry, American humorist, author, and journalist

G et off the sofa and do something around here!" Have you ever heard that statement from your wife before? What about this one: "Are you going to do something besides just sit there and watch sports all day?" That one is very popular among wives. You may actually hear worse or better, depending on your wife and her temperament. Maybe you hear those words now because when you lived with your mom, you heard these words: "That's okay, son, you can sleep all day. I'll do your laundry." Sound familiar? What about this one: "When you get home from work, I'll have dinner waiting for you." You get the picture here?

Just because that act worked with your mom doesn't mean it'll work with your wife. You're older and somewhat wiser now, and somewhere along the way you should've learned to do things on your own. Maybe it did carry over to married life, and nothing has changed. So grow up!

That's why if you ask most women what they want from their husbands, it's not tons of money, a big house, cars, or even hot, passionate sex. It's actually help around the house and assistance with the kids, mixed in with some unconditional love. That other stuff is great, but most of it doesn't last. That's when you turn to the stuff that makes a relationship ironclad. They're simple things that should come naturally, but somehow you've made them seem like a big deal. Either that or you do your best to ignore them. You feel that if you can pay someone else to do the job, you should. Your wife, however, wants you to save the money and roll up your sleeves and get a little sweaty. She doesn't need a momma's boy or even a little boy. If you don't know how to do something, she'll teach you. Then, when your mom comes over, you can tell her you helped clean. She'll either be proud to call you her son or mad at you for never doing it at her house when you lived there.

These ideas seek to uncover the ugly truth about men and our lack of skills when it comes to doing handyman work around the house. They will also help convert you, Mr. Lazy, into Mr. Home Improvement. What form of Mr. Home Improvement? It's up to you. Do you need a crash course in Tools 101, or can you tell the difference between a Phillips screwdriver and a flat-head? More importantly, if you've ever described a machine or tool by saying, "That weird looking squiggly thing-a-mah-jiggy," you may need some major help. If you don't know what all the parts of a vacuum cleaner do, what type of trash bags you need to handle used diapers (extra strength, by the way), or what cleaning product gets up baby food once it's thrown up, this is the perfect time to ask your wife. I'm sure she knows.

If you have goats eating your lawn because you've never used a lawnmower, it's time to send them to the hills and go invest in one of the greatest inventions ever. If you've never done drywall, laid tile, installed carpet, planted something, removed paint, put shingles on a roof, used duct tape to fix everything, or steam cleaned the carpet, this will be an awakening. By the time you finish reading this chapter, you may be ready to go to the mothership of all home improvement: Home Depot. This place is known for educating and turning the weekend football watcher into a tool master. You'll literally be known as the master of your domain. You can brag to all the guys about the jobs you've done. Your wife may even let you get your own tool shed in the backyard.

My wife knows I'm still working on something as simple as hanging a photo. I can barely take a photo, much less put it in a frame and hang it up. The last time I tried to do this, I put eight holes in the wall before finding a stud. That may actually sound strange to you, especially if you don't know what a stud is. This has nothing to do with a good-looking man or horse breeding. If you need to anchor screws or nails in the wall, a wall stud is an upright two-by-four on the opposite side of the drywall. You can actually buy a stud finder for about $3. Anyway, I didn't have one the night I needed it, so I went on blind faith. After the eighth hole, I finally found the stud and hung the picture.

Thankfully, the picture covered all the holes in the wall, and my wife thought I was a genius. That is, of course, until she accidentally knocked the picture frame down one day and discovered what I had done. That's when I enrolled in the "Hi, my name is Joe Gumm, and I don't know how to use tools" class down at the local recreation center where we live. It's a place where men can go and find refuge among others who are also tool illiterate.

It was highly embarrassing because my father-in-law is the total opposite. He's not only a handyman, but he can also catch a fish, gut the fish, fry the fish, and then eat the fish. He can hunt bear, deer, turkey, dove, and elk, shoot them, hang them on the wall and in the process, hang a picture frame just as straight, *on the same wall.* I don't know who should feel more ashamed, me or the animal hanging on the wall? He doesn't do it to make me look bad. He just has more time than I do. Of course, that's what I keep telling myself.

He saw the sloppy job I performed on the wall, and my wife actually got him to fix it. That's when I was summoned to the class. That was years ago, and even today, I'm still not allowed to go near a hammer, nails, screwdriver, wrench, or even a bottle opener.

Look, home improvement techniques are as simple as cooking. You can either slap two pieces of bread around a big, fat piece of bologna and chow down on pig intestines, or you can take your time and make a really nice gourmet meal. You just have to follow the directions. The more you know, the better. The better your skills, the more projects you'll get assigned. It doesn't take a wood shop teacher to guide you through the process, just a little patience, time, lots of wood for the mess-ups, and a calm demeanor. If you get upset at every piece of wood you cut too short, every wall fixture you can't hang, every hole you put in a wall, every drop of paint you get on the floor, or any leak you make worse, join the club. We've all made mistakes. However, getting to the point where you're actually doing this stuff is what's important to your wife.

That's part of the training process. It doesn't stop until we're in the ground, six feet under. Even then, I know my wife will still be looking into my casket while she's weeping hysterically, wondering why I have a tie on that doesn't match the rest of my outfit. It all works together, the grooming, the home improvement, all of it. That's why she wants you to shake off the former you (the one that lived with the mother that did everything for him) and come correct with the new you. It may be hard at first, but with a little detox, you'll be fine. You never know when you'll need to expand your wife's closet due to all of those shoes, so before you get to the list, take this self-evaluation exam to see where your status is on home improvement and handyman work. Good luck, and don't even think about calling your mom to help you cheat. She can't do it for you.

What does H&G stand for?
- ☐ House and Garage
- ☐ Home and Garden
- ☐ Hut and Garden
- ☐ Home and Garage

A hammer is used to do what?

- ☐ Put holes in a wall
- ☐ Mess up sheet rock
- ☐ Nail something somewhere
- ☐ Smash bugs on the ground
- ☐ Hit you on the head when you make your wife angry
- ☐ All of the above

As of today, I do not have

- ☐ A tool box
- ☐ A work bench
- ☐ Anything that plugs in
- ☐ Any knowledge of home improvement or handyman work whatsoever
- ☐ A clue about helping my wife around the house
- ☐ All of the above

Reasons why I don't like handyman work

- ☐ My mom and dad didn't teach me, so I didn't learn
- ☐ I like wasting money and hiring other people when something breaks
- ☐ I failed shop class
- ☐ I'm too lazy to pick up a book and learn
- ☐ I don't like wearing a thick, heavy tool belt
- ☐ It interferes with my TV viewing schedule
- ☐ It will ruin my soft, pretty hands
- ☐ All the above

Reasons why you should like handyman work

- [ ] It would please my wife
- [ ] It would please my wife
- [ ] It would please my wife
- [ ] It would please my wife
- [ ] All the above

What is a wrench?

- [ ] A sudden sharp, forcible twist or turn
- [ ] An injury produced by twisting or straining
- [ ] A sudden tug at one's emotions; a surge of compassion or anguish
- [ ] A hand or power tool, often used for gripping, turning, or twisting
- [ ] All the above

I don't know how to

- [ ] Screw in a light bulb
- [ ] Fix a cracked window
- [ ] Unclog a toilet or sink
- [ ] Vacuum or sweep
- [ ] Do anything. I'm lazy and unworthy of being called a man.

These are some of the excuses I make up when my wife wants me to do house work

- [ ] "You do it; you're better at it than me"
- [ ] "Can't we just call someone?"

☐ "If I fix it, I'm going to spend a lot of money at Home Depot, therefore I might as well not fix it"

☐ "I'll get to it later" (*later* meaning *never*)

Other things I would rather do than home improvement and handyman work

☐ Eat lint

☐ Leave a tuna sandwich in a school locker for a week and then put my head in the locker and smell the wonderful aroma

☐ Have a knee ligament repaired when it's not injured

☐ Perform a comedy routine at a funeral for someone I don't even know

☐ Eat baby food

☐ Sit and watch the chess channel for eight hours straight

After I read this chapter on handyman work and home improvement, I hope to

☐ Start with something small and make a ruler

☐ Build a small tree house

☐ Build a small dog house

☐ Build an entertainment system for my 60-inch flat screen with surround sound

☐ Start helping my wife around the house with little things and then eventually build up to bigger things

No matter how you did on your quiz, performing sweaty, messy, dirty jobs isn't fun. We all know that. Whether they're in the house, out of the house, building a doghouse, or cleaning an outhouse, they're not very popular and seem to always need to be done. In addition, your wife is depending on you to help her get these projects completed. Together, with two brains and a lot of your brawn, I'm sure you can figure out how to make your house look like it's in top shape...all the time. At least that's what your wife is hoping for. *Happy homemaking!*

It's all about her idea #61: Clean out the garage

They're not the worst four words you ever could hear, but they are pretty close. "You are being audited," "The cable is out," and "I have a headache," are others that would certainly beat "Clean out the garage." Take an hour away from working out or surfing the Net, or even golfing, and finally organize the garage. You might be surprised what kind of hidden treasure you'll find. My wife and I organized ours years ago and actually found stuff we could stick in the attic. It'll stay up there for a while. We'll get it down a few years later, and then it'll end up back in the garage. It's one big circle of getting out and putting away.

It's all about her idea #62: Help with the garage sale

First, you have to clean out the garage. Once that's done, you're basically selling the junk you cleaned out, or what I like what to call *the scrap* (emphasis on *crap*) you paid way too much money for years earlier from vacation spots like Walt Disney World. The $19.95 Buzz Lightyear doll your son played with for ten minutes is now going for 35 cents. How pathetic! But, if it helps your wife pull her minivan into the garage a lot more easily, I say GREAT!!! Clear the path. It's half your stuff anyway, so get out there and sell, sell, sell. Don't leave it just for her.

If you've ever done a garage sale, you know these things can be crazy. People show up at 6:00 in the morning and don't leave until they've found the best bargains. This money could be going toward something big, so get on board and make all the money you can. If you have signs to put out, go do it. If you have tons of high-ticket items, you can put the prices on them. If you have heavy stuff people need help loading, you may need to be the mule that does it. Get your back ready. You don't want things to be messy and unorganized.

It's all about her idea #63: Get organized

This should happen once you perform #61 and #62. It usually does if you have a pile full of junk in the garage and you're actually running it over each time you pull your car in. It's one thing to have a garage sale, but if the stuff that's left doesn't get straightened up, it's just the same junk going back into the garage, just less of it. You'll find yourself accomplishing a lot more than usual once you've done this. Tools will be stacked up real nicely. Cleaning materials, paint, lawn-mower equipment, gas, biohazardous products, swimming equipment, and everything else left over from the garage sale will be stacked on shelves, shoved in closets, and hung on the wall. Your neighbors won't believe it when they drive by. They'll stop wondering if the person who lived in the garage moved out.

It's all about her idea #64: Fix the thing

No, not your brain—we're not sure that can be fixed. I'm talking about the leaking faucet, the loose door handle, the stopped-up drain; whatever it is, just go ahead and fix the darn thing already. Your wife may oversee all operations of the house, but you're the super. Get your tools out and figure out how to repair it. Even if you are exhausted from work, and it's something she wants you to do when you get home, at least give it a try. I'm sure she'll give you an "A" for trying before calling in the professionals.

It's all about her idea #65: Replace a light bulb

Ever trip over something and cut your Achilles tendon, or step on a shoe and sprain your ankle? That's what she does every time she has to walk into an area without light. Come on, guys, this is the easiest chore in the world; let's make a group effort to complete this mission when our wives ask. Grab a bulb out of the cabinet and screw it in. It's not rocket science. That little thing lights up an entire room, but your wife can't see because you've procrastinated. Just remember the rule when you do this: "Righty-tighty, lefty-loosey."

It's all about her idea #66: Clean up throw up

Remember that part in your wedding vows about being "in sickness and in health," to which you responded, "I do"? Here it is in all its glory. You didn't know you were going to be a janitor, did you? It doesn't even matter if it comes from your wife, kids, animals, or yourself—be a trooper and start mopping or scrubbing. Didn't you do this in college for your buddies at the frat house? It's not glamorous, but she would do it for you in a heartbeat. If she wouldn't do it for you, she may just grab you a bucket.

It's all about her idea #67: Make the yard look nice

Whether women live in a trailer or a mansion, I find that they always want their front yards to look nice. This is your time to shine and make her happier in the process. Sure, you don't have a green thumb and don't know the difference between lawn care and landscaping, but that doesn't matter. She just wants it looking nice and presentable. If you don't have time for yard work, find someone who does. Bushes and plants cost a little but shouldn't take too much time to plant. If in doubt, ask someone at the plant store what would work in your region and also be low maintenance. Sweat a little and act like you're John Deere. Get it done early and watch the game later. Even ask her to help. Most women don't mind working in the yard because they're burning calories and getting a tan all at the same time.

It's all about her idea #68: Clean her car

There's nothing worse than getting into a car and it smelling like someone or something died or like a science project in the making. Who knows what has been left in the car—milk, a tuna fish sandwich, fruit, or an actual body. Your wife may tow the children around a lot more than you do, so it may happen more often in her car. Quit spending all of your time spit shining your BMW and give her minivan a scrub down, inside and out. If the kids aren't around anymore, clean the car anyway. It's the unselfish guy code of never wanting to outdo your wife. That means if you walk into a room and people stare at her first, then you get husband credit for being a gentleman. The same goes for your cars. Make sure her car always looks better than yours, and if you share a car, just double-team the thing.

It's all about her idea #69: Plant flowers

How many hints does it take for you to catch on to this one? Every time you guys go by the neighbor's house, she mentions it. Pink, red, purple, orange, or yellow, buy a bundle, a few, a truckful or one. Flowers aren't bushes or trees or bigger than your hand, so it shouldn't take too long or be too messy. The yard looks great, but think about how much nicer it'll look with some color. This is not hard, and it's far away from a hammer and wall.

It's all about her idea #70: Build a fire

This could be done outside while camping or indoors while hanging out relaxing. (Of course, only if you have a fireplace. Don't start one in the middle of your floor for no reason.)

Most women don't want that good-looking, six-packed, long-haired beefcake on the front cover of romance novels or magazines. They want a William Wallace character to come rescue them from the daily grind of house work, kids, and family, someone who can hunt down a large animal and kill it with his bare hands, come home and put it on the grill, and serve it up on a plate. Since you're not him and will never have a six-pack unless it's in the form of sodas, do something that's real instead. This is as real as it gets.

Light the fire, get your wife, go to your nearest sofa, and start your own fire. Throw on some Marvin Gaye, and you'll definitely heat things up. Either that or you'll sweat, put out the fire, take a shower to clean off the sweat, put on some cooler clothes, throw the matches away, and never build a fire again.

It's all about her idea #71: Do the one chore she's been bugging you to do forever

Clean the gutters, fix the leak, hang the shelves, rake the leaves, put the knob back on the door, or change the oil in her car. Whatever it is—just do it. It's obviously frustrating her and making something look ugly. Do it so your father-in-law doesn't have to come over and make you look less significant than you already are.

It's all about her idea #72: Take your muddy shoes off before you come into the house

If you love getting on your hands and knees wiping up the mud you dragged in, keep your shoes on. You may have thought this one belonged in the first four chapters, but once you do this, you may have to figure out how to clean it up. I know we don't live in Asia, where it's customary to remove your shoes when entering a home, but she's made this request a hundred and fifty thousand times, and you're still not doing it. Ever wonder why your carpet is dirty? You're dragging your big, fat, shoe-clad feet across the floor every time you come in from work, mowing the yard, shooting hoops, and jogging, that's why. Just take the shoes off already. Your stinky feet are probably more bearable than what is underneath your shoe anyway. If you do get mud on the carpet, would you know how to clean it up? Carpet cleaner may not be the answer. If you create a mess enough times, you may have to rent a carpet steamer and clean the entire house. Take the dirty shoes off so you can avoid doing some major home improvement.

It's all about her idea #73: Paint

Believe it or not, there's an actual art to this, and not all people are capable of staying in the lines. I realized this years ago when my wife and I settled into three different houses in a span of five years. Up until then, the only thing I had ever painted was a piece of art. I was so bad that on the first house I didn't even get to help out. In the second house, I got paint on the ceiling and the floor, and just about ruined one room completely. In the third house, my wife didn't even want me to participate; I was that bad. Evidently, you're supposed to put tape on the crown molding and at the bottom and tops of the walls. I never did that. I also didn't use the right paint or the right color or put enough on. It's an actual process that needs to be thought out and looked at before starting. So the next time I paint anything, I'll know to ask a professional beforehand. I'll also make sure there's more on the wall than on me.

It's all about her idea #74: Know your terms so you'll be prepared

When your wife suddenly calls you out of the clear blue at work and sounds excited because she wants to "gut something," don't freak out. It doesn't necessarily mean it's a pig or even a family member. It basically means she's had time to think about taking the guts out of something in your house and doing something different. It could be a room, a ceiling, the landscaping in the backyard, the restroom, or the entire house. To "gut something" isn't so bad, but watch out for words like *remodel, patch, makeover, build, install, replace, recycle, renovate, restore, add,* and *repair*. When you're at dinner or a movie and your wife uses one of these words, you'll know what you are getting yourself into. If you agree, have several contractors come in and give you an estimate. That will at least give you an idea of what you're looking at financially.

It's all about her idea #75: Make something

Not a mess, of course. Something that makes sense to her. It doesn't matter if it's a one-book bookshelf or a toothpick, every man should make something at least once in his life just to be able to say, "I built something." If you've never felt the force of a power tool in your hand, you're missing out on something great. My in-laws have a lot of nice furniture in their home, but the focal point is the piece my father-in-law made with his own two hands. (He's not a carpenter but certainly could be one.) That table gets all the magazines, the glasses that leave rings, and the toys from the grandchildren resting on top of it. He also revamped our computer desk, built several pieces of furniture for our house, put together a playhouse for my daughter, and actually built a cabin. I, on the other hand, have actually used a toothpick and sharpened a pencil. Do I have some work to do to catch up to him? Yes. Will I ever catch up to someone like him? Probably not. That's okay. That's why my wife married me, because she knew her dad could do all of that. However, I am building up my tool chest, and maybe one day I'll be able to take on some major project—like building a birdhouse.

Chapter Eight

Pretty Major Stuff

"Freud died at age eighty-three still asking one question: 'What do women want?'"

—Bette Midler's character to Mel Gibson's character
in the movie *What Women Want*

Remember your wedding day? Depending on when it was, you may recall some details. Your wife, on other hand, remembers every last moment, even the part when her father got up at the reception and toasted the wedding party by saying, "I spent $70,000 on my daughter's college education. I thought she was smarter than this."

She could probably also quote your vows verbatim and sing each song from the evening. Women love talking about that stuff with other women. That's why it's always good to know what you did at the altar in front of God, family, friends, the minister, or the judge. In most traditional weddings, there's a part about honoring your wife. There's also a part about loving her with commitment and devotion, and respecting her at all times. That means the boring, the funny, the wild, the goofy, the hot, the cold, the big, the little, the harsh, the everything. It's like the fine print at the end of a contract or agreement that no one reads. It's the "Terms and Conditions" part. It's the thing you have to scroll down the page to see. There's so much small print, you don't have time to read it. You agree to the deal and find out later you should have had your lawyer take a look-see. So when you ask yourself, "Did I really sign up for this? Did I really agree to this?" the answer is a resounding, *yes!*

I'm not talking about the stuff you discuss when you first started dating your wife or when you got engaged. That's called ooey-gooey, pre-marriage fluff. I'm talking about all the hard-core, in-your-face, heavy-duty substance that builds a history between you and your wife. Fond memories that last and make up the fiber of a relationship, things like chicken pox, your kids' elementary school crushes, pets dying, cars breaking down, plumbing problems, home repairs, insurance issues, mortgages, floods, bounced checks, bills, bankruptcy, in-laws, outlaws, spills on the carpet, arguments, sickness, lost remote controls (very important), and depression. These are the kind of things that make marriage really interesting. Add kids to that, and you'll really have some fun.

Take a minute to think about the day you returned from your honeymoon. Or, if you didn't take a honeymoon, think about the day after you were married. Which one was scarier, the day you got married or the day after? And when I say *scary*, I mean anxious and curious about the future and not knowing what the next day will bring, not *scary* as in, "Uh oh! I think I just made the biggest mistake of my life." Those questions in your head start piling on one after another. Will there be a nest egg for those "just in case" moments? Are kids in the picture? What if we're pregnant right now? Did I marry the right person? What if I lose my job tomorrow? Am I ever going to get along with her family? What if she divorces me? What if she throws a burrito at me? Will I get caught for all of those towels I stole from our honeymoon hotel? Those are definitely the types of questions we all think about once we tie the knot.

So what's the key to survival once you get past those questions? I couldn't tell you, and I really don't think anyone can. I think it depends on whom you ask and what situation they're in. Some would say love, some would say communication, some would say passion, some would say family—the list is endless. Up and down moments happen every day during marriage—we all go through tough times. I think it's how we get past the up and down moments that counts, even if the ooey-gooey isn't there anymore. All of that time and energy we had to be ooey-gooey is now used for other ventures in life—like kids.

That's when the hair turns gray or goes bye-bye forever, you gain twice as much weight, you lose half the sleep you once had, you're on a twenty-four-hour-a-day heartburn watch because of two little things called stress and worry, you lose your hearing, you have more headaches and ulcers and moments of memory loss, and it's never quiet in your house ever, ever, ever, ever again. Okay, maybe just a few hours a night, because they'll get tired sometime, but it's definitely not like it was before kids.

Then they will have kids, and that means grandkids for you. They'll be running down the same halls your kids ran down, screaming and laughing and hollering and hooting. With your own children, you'll see and experience drama and excitement like you've never seen before. You may have already gone through it or are going through it right now. Whichever it is, no doubt you've experienced what other men have experienced, including the emotional roller coaster kids like to ride every minute of every hour of every day of your entire life. It's the ride at the relationship park that they never take a break from.

All along, you've been wondering about that part in your wedding vows that said, "Till death do us part." This is it. On most days, it will seem as if you're actually dying, but not because you may think your kids are out to get you, though it may seem like that at times (especially when your three-year-old is throwing a major fit in the middle of a mall, a restaurant, or in the foyer of church in front of the minister). The energy that they suck out of your body is one thing. Combine that with the other stuff at the beginning of this chapter, and you understand what I mean when I say, "Till death do us part." This isn't a bad thing. It's just a human thing, a couple thing, a shared experience. That's why there's supposed to be two of you, a mommy and a daddy, a double team, two on one, or two on two, or even two on three or four sometimes.

Some couples say it really doesn't matter if you have boys or if you have girls, but I'm partial to girls because I have four. I think, though, that girls may be a little more emotional when it comes to acting out their feelings and what they're thinking. That's just my opinion. It may not be a popular one, especially with men who have boys; they may be just as emotional.

In fact, with all the females in my house, we could win for

"Best Drama" at the Academy Awards every year. Many times when I call my wife at home and ask her how her day has been, she will say, "Busy." I know exactly what that means. My girls are up and about and having all kinds of fun making stuff and creating messes for my wife.

Of course, before we had four girls, my wife and I always talked about having children and how we would rear them. As you well know, the image you have before marriage and the image you have after you have kids is totally different. We imagined our family portrait would look something like *Little House on the Prairie*. Our girls would roam the western countryside of Minnesota, frolicking with our dog and churning cheese with Ma (that would be my wife). I would be a homesteader finding work at the local mill. It obviously didn't end up that way (because this isn't the 1870s) and usually doesn't for most families. I think we all end up looking more like the Munsters—a lot of zaniness, crazy characters, and kooky times.

That's what this chapter is all about. It's about looking past the stress, worry, anxiety, and somewhat crazy times of marriage and family, and making the best of it. Sure, it would've been nice to have a warning before marriage and kids that got us all prepared for the worst and the best. You know, the ones that pharmaceutical companies use when they're trying to market a pill on TV? Of course, the side effects would have been a little different: "This product may cause upset stomachs, disoriented speech, nausea, back pain, blurred vision, weeping (maybe a lot of it), loss of bladder control, hurt feelings, and joint pain."

Unfortunately, we didn't get one. That's okay. We press on and figure out what's next. I know it sounds simple to say, but everyone goes through the same experiences you do. We may have different wives and kids, live in different cities, go to different schools, attend different churches, and have different beliefs, but we all walk in similar shoes. Rich or poor, black or white, cold or hot, fun, loud, big and small, you signed on the dotted line when you agreed to marriage. The pressure is now on for you to step up to the plate and knock one out of the park, the same way you do at work in the boardroom. You handle pressure and problems with grace, poise, and composure. Quit being a poser; use the same technique at home, and you'll be fine.

It's all about her idea #76: Be kind and understanding during PMS

This comes once a month, twelve times a year, and it's not your *Sports Illustrated* magazine subscription. It's your wife's monthly cycle. And right before it is PMS. We all know what this is. It's a little acronym that represents some Pretty Major Stuff in the life of your wife. Not only does your wife have to deal with you and your children on a daily basis, she also has to cope with surging hormones that affect her emotions and general feeling of well-being. Despite the fact that her emotions may change, don't you change. She may have more ups and downs than the Dow or the S&P. That's when she's depending on you the most to step up. Don't blow it by saying something stupid. Of course,

PMS is just one of the many acronyms your wife has to keep balanced in her life while going through this. She's the CEO of your home. She attends PTA meetings and discusses your child (the one with ADHD) with the teacher and must be dealt with ASAP. Of course, all the while, you feel like you're DOA when you get home from work, so instead of going to that PTA meeting with your wife, you hit the couch and watch ESPN on your HDTV while checking out the new DVD you just purchased, *ET*. Be a gentleman, be brave, take one for the home team, buy her some chocolate brownies, and be thankful you aren't a woman in the USA. My advice, use some TLC and you should be A-OK.

It's all about her idea #77: Help her do the Christmas cards

Next to hell, filling out insurance forms, being audited, and getting a root canal, I would say this is next in line. Why? Mainly because some women make it that way, or at least my wife does. I say that not because I want to die, but because here we are celebrating the most joyous occasion on the planet, Christmas, and the birth of our Lord and Savior Jesus Christ, and my wife has chosen picture time to be the most stressed out. It doesn't make sense. This is supposed to be a happy occasion, right? Then why do I feel as if getting punched in the crotch would make me feel better?

One particular time, she not only bought the outfits in October, but we took the pictures in October. Not Halloween photos, Christmas photos. Not Thanksgiving pictures, Christmas pictures…in October. "Well, she wanted to plan ahead and make sure she got them done," some would say, and they would be right. The problem was, she had way too much time to think about ALL of the things she didn't like about the pictures, so she went out and bought new outfits for the kids and we shot our Christmas pictures again, in November. And again, she was unhappy with the result.

That's when I found out her unhappiness took shape in the form of flavors, some people call them moods: happy, sad, stressed, worried, mad, glad, and indifferent. They come in all different types of shapes and sizes.

This card may seem like the most minute thing to you, but to your wife it's the world. No joke, it's literally the world. That's how many she plans on sending out—enough for the entire world. Sure, there are more important things you could be doing in the month of October—that's when most women start preparing for this exciting family craft. She orders the cards. If you have kids, she has to pick out the perfect outfits that match. She has to choose the photographer. She has to book a date. She has to get her hair done. She has to figure out who's going to get a card. Then she has to address the envelopes.

It's called work, and believe it or not, women enjoy this. If we were in charge of this, no one would ever get that yearly reminder of what our family looks like. Of course, after all the hard work is done and the cards are sent out, they're still not one hundred percent happy with the result. You either gave a fake smile, your two-year-old was crying, your dog's sweater was a different shade of red than your shirt, her hair was curly and not straight, or the cards were three and a half by five and she wanted a four by six. It really doesn't matter if they turned out to be perfect, women will spend the next ten months of the year talking, preparing, and getting ready to do it all over again. If you can also help her decorate the house with Christmas decorations, this would almost be bigger than the card thing. If you don't do any of the above, you may just find your chestnuts roasting on an open fire. If you decide to give her a hand, she may take full advantage of the mistletoe.

It's all about her idea #78: Bring in the groceries

Good for you; you didn't have to go to the grocery store with your wife because she let you stay home to watch college football. Fine. So now that she's home with the groceries, why not help her bring them in? She bought $200 worth, and she has a ton of bags, including several with canned goods. That's a workout in itself. Go all the way with this one. Not only should you help her bring them in, but you should also help her put them away.

It's all about her idea #79: Let her know about the finances

Be honest about the bills. If you're poor, tell her you're poor. She'll probably hate it, but at least she'll know the truth. So many women are taken off guard because they're not sure what's in the bank. You may die one day unexpectedly, and she may not know where everything is. Sit her down, show her everything you guys have, and get her up to speed. She may be a littler smarter in the bookkeeping department than you think. She actually may be better than you. (If you have already handed over the reins to the checkbook, give yourself a pat on the back.)

It's all about her idea #80: Watch the kids when your wife works out

Hey, you might as well. You're plopping down tons of money for her gym membership; she might as well take advantage. Plus, there are two benefits to this: 1.) Your wife feels good because she's working on getting the perfect body, and 2.) you're able to bond with your children. This is the time for your wife to get away from everything. It's her free time, emphasis on *free*. No boss, no kids, no pressure, no stress, no rules, no games, no phones, no worries. There are two certainties to married life with kids: Men are interested in what their wife's rear looks like, and women are interested in rearing the children. It works out for everybody. If she can work out during the day while you're at work, it's a plus. If she can't, help her find the time to do it at night.

It's all about her idea #81: Eat at the dinner table

Your wife spent all afternoon getting a nice dinner prepared for the family, and you want to watch that episode of *Everybody Loves Raymond* you've seen fifty times. Turn off the TV, and sit with your wife and kids, and have that special bonding time with the family. This is the time everyone wants to tell Daddy about their day. If it's just you and your wife, then it should give you plenty of time to discuss whatever you want without any distractions from kids. If things get quiet, you could probably even get by with talking about the *Everybody Loves Raymond* episode; just make sure it's at the dinner table.

It's all about her idea #82: Feed the animals

These would be actual pets, not your kids. Your wife has her hands full with munchkins of the human kind, and you were the one who approved getting the dog in the first place. You may have a cat that sheds, claws the furniture, and even scratches visitors, or it could be a dog that howls at night, makes messes during the day, drools, and drags mud into the house, the same house your wife is trying to keep clean with kids running around. She already has to deal with you and the children. She doesn't need to compete with a forty-five-pound slobbering furball or a feline that purrs louder than you snore. The least you can do is make sure they're getting adequately fed. This doesn't mean leftovers from the table.

It's all about her idea #83: Grocery shop with her

Don't like the brand of ice cream, chips, cereal, batteries, or toilet paper your wife's getting you when she goes to the store? Get off your rump and go with her—or better yet, go yourself. Just make sure to get specific instructions so you don't buy the wrong brand. Whoever said going to the store was her job anyway? No one. Many men just assume that if women don't go to the store and actually pick up the groceries, life would end. That's probably true, but if you can read a list, you can certainly do it once, twice, or all of the time.

It's all about her idea #84: Fill her car up with gas

There's nothing worse than your wife being in a rush to work or getting the kids to school and not having enough gas. Your wife has to stop and refuel, she doesn't have her makeup on, and now she gets to smell like petrol the rest of the day. Check the tank at night or ask if she needs gas. This isn't a huge handyman job, but it's certainly one your wife wouldn't mind having done for her.

It's all about her idea #85: Transfer all of the family videos

It's a complete pain in the rear, but what's going to be less painful, hearing your wife cry and complain about it when she doesn't have anything to watch to remind her of the good old days, or transferring the videos?

What are you waiting for, the kids to be grown up and out of the house? Do it now. You've spent years taking video of the kids' special moments but have nothing to show for it. Quit playing solitaire on your computer and make some memories. No matter what their ages, your kids are sure to love watching themselves on the big screen. Why get a video camera if you're not going to turn the footage into special memories? Remember, that's why you spent all of that time recording their plays, baseball games, dances, prom dates, birthday parties, and class outings. When the kids are all out of the house, this may be the one thing that keeps your wife sane.

It's all about her idea #86: Iron something

Maybe if you can't afford professional cleaning right now, this is the way to go. It's not the worst thing on the planet, but it could be embarrassing when your boss says, "Sleep in your shirt last night, Bob?" Get out the iron, plug it in, add water for steam, and get the wrinkles out by yourself. Your wife is not your personal laundry service. She's just as busy as you are in the morning. It was your fault you forgot to take that shirt to the cleaners, and now you need it for the meeting today. It's not chemical engineering. Depending on how terrible the wrinkles are, I'm sure it's just a few strokes back and forth. Your twelve-year-old daughter can probably teach you if you need help. Just don't ask her in the morning; she's in line to iron that tank top she wants to wear to school.

It's all about her idea #87: Plan a vacation

The location, the dates, the travel agency—take the initiative on everything from the smallest item to the biggest luxury. It can be a resort vacation, a cruise, a trip to Europe, a trip within the United States, a vacation to the beach, a city getaway, a road trip, or a camping vacation. You can plan it with the kids or without the rascals, even let the grandparents tag along. The point is, no matter how busy you are, block off a span of time to get this done.

It's all about her idea #88: Wrap a present

Okay, it's very girly sounding, and on top of that, it feels feminine. Let me clarify—this doesn't mean having it wrapped. It means doing it yourself. Spending time on finding a gift for your wife is great, but when you take the time to wrap it yourself, she'll appreciate that almost more than the gift. (Ultimately, this will depend on what the gift is.) If you don't have wrapping paper around the house, go to your local gift shop. If you don't have a local gift shop, go to the local gas station, buy a newspaper for fifty cents, read it, and then use it for wrapping paper. If it's a fabulous gift, you may fool her by making her think she's getting something that's as worthy as the wrapping paper. Also, if she needs help wrapping gifts for Christmas, birthdays, or special occasions, you'll be prepared.

It's all about her idea #89: Quit whining about being injured or hurt

I stopped doing this the second I saw my oldest daughter come out of my wife's birth canal. Let's admit it, when you stub a toe, it hurts. Slamming a hand in the car door, getting a paper cut, a hammer to the thumb, these are all good reasons to cry, whine, or let out a big, loud moan. But don't ever make it obvious or overdo it in front of a woman. It's sort of an unknown rule. If you do it, you'll probably get zero affection and actually be embarrassed. Try to explain to a woman why your little hurt toe is more painful than a baby coming out of her pelvis. You can't and should never do it. I will never understand why men use the phrases, "Don't be such a woman," or "You're such a woman," when referring to how a man handles pain. It must be a compliment.

It's all about her idea #90: Buy her that one thing she's always wanted

It could be an antique clock, tickets to the zoo, china, a trip to China, a cell phone, a plasma TV, or a minivan. You've put it off forever, and now you're looking to give it to her for a birthday gift, a Christmas gift, or Valentine's Day. Figure out a good time to give it to her (at the office in front of her coworkers), maybe even involve the children. No doubt, your wife's heart will be full of glee. If your children are grown, do it with the grandkids.

Chapter Nine

Quit Acting like You're "The Man" and Actually Be "The Man"

"Lovemaking begins in the kitchen with men helping their wives."

—Dr. James Dobson, author and founder of
Focus on the Family

For centuries, men have promoted slothfulness, irresponsibility, and procrastination by using two sentences their wives hate hearing: "In a minute," and "I'll do it later." It has helped get them out of more work, cleaning, jobs around the house, trips to the grocery store, and lawn care. This can only be blamed on one thing and one thing alone: sports. That's why those words have never really been accepted by the female persuasion. By nature, women are more aggressive than men when it comes to getting things done. They're sharper, more attentive, prepared, and organized, and are awesome multitaskers. They have to be. We need to be. When they say they want it done now, by golly, they'll find a way to get it done, by hell or high water and without the help of their husbands.

That's why when you say, "I'll get it done later," your wife gets inspired and does great things. You, on the other hand, are a glorified couch potato. Why not step out of that rut and get on board the active train. Your wife's the conductor and is looking for you to bring up the caboose or at least get your lazy caboose off the couch. You don't ever want your wife to sing that little ditty that goes, "Daddy, Daddy, he's our man, if he can't do it, Grandpa can." Cut the laziness and get to work. You don't want to be known as the son-in-slacker, do you?

I've learned over the past few years that there are literally hundreds of little tasks my wife will make up for me to do. If she doesn't have any, she'll invent some. These aren't necessarily chores around the house; they're also around the city and the state. They range from going to the store and picking up skin foundation (this is the makeup base they put on their faces) to making reservations at a bed and breakfast four hours away from where we live. They're miniscule things now, but they weren't when we first got married.

When my wife and I first got married, I really didn't notice it that much because the marriage was fresh and clean and pure and just downright, throw-up sickening. That's how much we were in love. You know what kind of love I'm talking about, the ridiculous and annoying, school-kid, giddy love. It's so openly mushy and gooey that old married couples just want to laugh because they know that type of love is more lust-motivated. That's how bad it was, and that's how it should be for newly-weds. We would do anything for each other, at any moment, and anywhere. I was actually worse than she was. I was like her little robot. She could control me anyway she wanted. I would do things like clean the attic in 105-degree Texas heat, tar the driveway, put up a new fence, and even sod the entire yard.

As the years went by, I noticed the errands weren't as elaborate. Don't get me wrong; there were still things she wanted me to do for her, but they weren't as demanding physically or as difficult. These were smaller tasks: an oil change for her car, picking up her prescription at the drug store, taking the pictures in to get developed, marking things on the calendar, helping move something around the house, or taxiing the kids to an event. I was definitely her little errand boy. One day it, hit me. What am I doing? I should be watching a game or hanging out with the guys or catching a flick. I realized at that point that I was spending all my time doing stuff for her. I mentioned it one day while I was cleaning underneath our sink (something else I was coerced into doing). As I took another strong whiff of chemical cleaner, I said to her, "What am I doing?" She then replied, with a giggle and slight sarcasm, "You're being my little slave boy. Now get back to work."

I sat there for the next hour thinking about leaving, and going out and doing something I wanted to do. *I* didn't want to spend my weekends doing odd jobs around the house. I wanted to do stuff that other men were doing on Saturdays, like go to the lake or fish or play in a softball tournament. Then I thought to myself, *I don't have a boat, I don't like fishing because the worms are slimy and I can't ever get them on the hook, and I'm not on a softball team.* Plus, to be honest, I loved hanging out with my wife and kids on weekends. It didn't matter if I was cleaning the sink, digging a ditch, putting insulation in the attic, or cleaning carpets. The joy came from seeing my wife happy because I was helping her out with her list, no matter what it entailed. Of course, the lists always got longer and longer.

You don't know how it happens. You don't when it happens. All of a sudden, one day, you're sitting there watching *SportsCenter*, and the next day you're peeling a mango for the fruit salad your wife's making. You then find yourself at work talking about the new crock pot you got, and your coworkers start wondering if you need a shot of testosterone.

Some of the stuff may not even have to do with your wife. It may be stuff you need to do with or for your children. We all remember those days of science fair projects. In eighth grade, I waited until the final night to get mine done. For three months prior, I couldn't think of anything to do, so with the help of my parents, some tape and glue, some plants, rock music, and fast thinking, I was able to put together a well-done, C-plus project the night before it was due. It was aptly named, "The effects of rock music on plants." It was the lamest piece of junk ever produced for Mr. Edwards's science class.

Of course, when I got to school the next morning, he put me between two A students' projects. There I was with a wimpy piece of foam core with papers barely hanging on, and the two people beside me had wooden storyboards put together with hinges. They had professional-looking drawn graphs with detailed information they had gathered through months of preparation. My project explained how plants were affected by the types of rock music played to them for hours and hours. One plant was wilted; the other wasn't. It was that simple. I didn't have a battery-operated anything or a volcano flowing with lava.

I did learn a valuable lesson, however. No, it wasn't the lesson about not waiting until the last minute to do something. I still do that today. It was the lesson about love I got from my parents, who helped me stay up late that night putting the thing together. Not only did I get it done, I eventually passed my science class, and that's really what they were hoping for anyway.

Little, big, huge, or gigantic, the "little things" in life that turn out to be bigger than what you expected are the things your wife needs help with, especially if it has to do with the kids. Women want things done. That's what their lives are fueled by. It's not sleeping, it's not eating, it's not getting rewarded for their work or receiving praise for a job well done. We all know women certainly deserve and like hearing "thank you" every once in a while, but what women long for more than anything is to accomplish the things that need to be taken care of on a daily basis. You can call them lists, honey dos, reminders, whatever you want. If you're not helping, then step aside, because you're probably hurting. Once she forgets about something or gets off track, she may lose focus and blame you for it. You don't want that. Hell hath no fury like a woman who is scorned and/or loses focus on a "to do" list.

It's all about her idea #91: Call her at home or at work just because

I know this sounds like you're checking in, but it's not that at all. Checking in is what my dad wanted me to do when I was fifteen and started dating girls. He always said, "Wherever you go, just make sure you always call me before you come home." I loved that rule because he never went to sleep until I called. I would call him and tell him I was coming home, and he would go straight to bed. My thinking was, I would eventually get home that night—I just wasn't heading home at that exact time. He never picked up on it, but he will obviously be disappointed and angered when he reads this.

But this is different. You're calling your wife to see how her day has been. That's all. Nothing more, nothing less. It's just a quick contact to see how her day is going. You're not snooping on her either. There's no official rule that says you have to check in, but no doubt she'll be happy to hear your voice.

It's all about her idea #92: Ask for directions

Or get a GPS. This isn't the time to be stubborn. Yes, the MO for most men is that we don't do this. Just pull over already and break the mold. You've been lost for hours and now you're really late. Don't blame it on your wife either. She told you to go online and look up directions on mapquest.com or yellowpages.com.

You didn't do it, so now you're missing out on a wedding, a funeral, a graduation, a dinner reservation, a dedication, or maybe even an important sporting event. You don't want to get stuck in the middle of nowhere or on a major thoroughfare. Didn't you see the movie *Deliverance*? Way to go, Mr. Mapsco. Put aside your bullheaded stubbornness for one night and stop at the nearest gas station.

It's all about her idea #93: Don't go to a place for dinner that has a television playing sports

You might as well stay at home if that's going to happen. Your wife wants your full attention during dinner. First of all, she's been at work all day, either at home or at an office (both jobs are important, and in case you were wondering, working at home is often harder). Secondly, she's looking for some adult time with you. Thirdly, she shouldn't have to compete with Shaquille O'Neal, Tom Brady, or Alex Rodriguez. Pay attention to her. If you're having trouble finding a place without a TV, try to locate an Amish restaurant. They won't know what *SportsCenter* is.

It's all about her idea #94: Be punctual

This sounds really close to *punch you out*, which she's liable to do if you're late again. Or just change the spelling to *PUNK-tual*, because that's what you're being when you tell her you'll be there in twenty minutes and it ends up being forty minutes. When you say twenty minutes, mean it. If it's going to be an hour, call her and let her know. Time is of the essence. The kids may have to be somewhere, dinner may be cooked and on the table, your wife may be pregnant and her water almost breaking—you never know why you may be needed. That's why it's always better to be early than late. If you're late running, give her a call.

It's all about her idea #95: Set goals with your wife

This could mean planning for your financial future, retirement, college funds, a family vacation, a second honeymoon, a new career, a new car, a new house, or paying off a huge bill. Write your goals down together and stick with them. Most couples are too busy talking about what they want to do instead of taking steps toward completion. Go the distance, follow through, and be proud when you do.

It's all about her idea #96: Turn on whatever music she wants in the car

Toby Keith, T-Pain, the guy from *American Idol* with his pants on the ground, and even Justin Bieber are all great musicians, but for the love of being tone deaf, let your wife listen to something else. You occupy the car more than she does, and most of the time you probably listen to sports talk, so let her play her Michael Bublé. If she can bear your eighties rock falsetto in the shower, you can listen to her music in the car.

It's all about her idea #97: Skip watching sports for a day

Compared to taking Christmas pictures, making the bed, scrapbooking, and having a conversation with your mother-in-law about being a better father and husband, this isn't really a big deal. Go to the mall with her; Sure it's fun to fool around on the computer, watch the ball game, or even go check out a flick at the theater on your day off, but why not pick a weekend and go hang out with your wife at the local shopping village? You guys can shop for clothes, shoes, purses (just for her—not for you), and even grab some of that delicious food at the local cafe. You can Tivo all the sports you want and watch them when you get home. Remember, it's just for a weekend or two, not every weekend.

It's all about her idea #98: If she works outside the home, surprise her on a lunch break

She'll likely brag about this surprise lunch to her work buddies and coworkers for months. You showing up and whisking her off to lunch in front of all the people she has to work with everyday (preferably with roses in hand), what could be more heroic? She'll be the envy of all her friends. And the good part is you may not even have to go to lunch (hint, hint). Better yet, if she works at home, skip a lunch with the guys to go hang out with her.

It's all about her idea #99: Remember a date that you may have thought was insignificant

The first kiss, the first time you met, your first date—nothing would be more impressive to your wife than if you knew one of these. Not just remembering the date of the event, but remembering details and commemorating it in a special way. I remember when my wife called me at work one day and said, "Happy anniversary." With slight hesitancy, I responded back with a question, "You, too?" I wasn't sure what she was talking about. I did the memory file cabinet check of all of the important dates. I thought, *My goodness, I can't even remember my own anniversary, how pathetic.* Then I thought about leaving work early, stopping somewhere to get her a gift, and booking reservations at our favorite restaurant. Talk about panicking. I came to find out it was the anniversary of the first time we kissed— underneath the moonlight while our favorite song was playing in the background as we leaned up against my car. What gift do you get her for that? I went out and bought her some lipstick, a CD, car wax, and a new outfit. She didn't get me anything. The point is, women remember every little date and outing you go on. Try to remember at least one. (But I've learned not to go so crazy on the gifts.)

It's all about her idea #100: Quit wasting money you can't afford to waste

This would include spending money on any form of gambling, like the lottery or horse racing, as well as cigarettes, car accessories, expensive glasses, stereo equipment, computer games, movie rentals, magazines, alcohol, etc. When you do this, don't ever gripe again about your wife spending money on shoes, purses, high-end makeup, or anything else expensive. Your kid needs braces, but here you are smoking two packs of cigarettes a day.

Even if it's two packs a week, that is still money not going to the new shoes or college fund. Use all the dough on the family, or train yourself to put it away for a rainy day. (Do some fun things, too, but do them as a family.) If you have kids, you'll have plenty of rainy days. Stop the impulse buying and get back on track. Of course, if you win the $100 million state jackpot, I'm sure your wife will forgive you. If you're not a millionaire, able to spend at will, buying anything you want, and you're an impulse buyer of junk, give the duties to your wife to run the bank. The less you have, the more that goes back into your family.

It's all about her idea #101: See a movie she wants to see

Hearing the "F" word fifty-three times in a Quentin Tarantino movie is quite pleasing to the ears, but every time you go to the theater, does it always have to be guns, blood, cursing, and things blowing up? Have you not seen enough of all of that with your kids at home? It's either that, a sports movie, or a vulgar comedy. Try drama, suspense, or maybe even a tear-jerker she wants to see. Try alternating like my wife and I do. We have kids, so going to a theater is about as likely as the Publisher's Clearing House van showing up at our door, but when we get a chance to do it, we'll either see a movie we both want to watch or take turns choosing. Usually, during a movie I want to watch, my wife will spend the whole time asking me, "What did he just say?" Of course, then I have to spend the next thirty seconds explaining to her what the actor said. Right after I do that, we'll both miss the current dialogue, and she'll then lean over and say, "What did he just say right there?" I'll reply sharply, "I don't know what he just said because you were yapping in my ear with your popcorn breath." It's just as fun when we go see a movie she wants to see. I usually get some good sleep or catch up on getting higher scores on my cell phone video games. One of my friends was about to go see a sob-fest movie with his wife and actually asked her why she wanted to see a movie that made her cry and get all stressed out. She answered, "Because I would rather do it at the movie theater than at home with you." Point well taken.

It's all about her idea #102: Wife and kids versus cell phone

First of all, it's not even a fair fight. Your wife and kids could demolish your tiny, little cell phone. And, that's probably what they'll end up doing if you keep texting during dinner. If you ask most women, they would probably tell you that men have abused some of today's greatest inventions. Some of the more famous ones would include the remote control, the microwave, digital video recorders, video game machines, cars, CD players, computers, and the worst of all, cell phones. Of course, if you ask my wife, she would probably say I've abused my hair straightener. Anyway, back in 1967, researchers looked at crude mobile (car) phones and realized that by using small cells with frequency reuse they could increase the traffic capacity of mobile phones substantially. Now the technology is getting better, and we're getting more idiotic with the use of them.

"Does mine have a camera on it?" "Can it take pictures?" "Does mine play games?" "Does mine have a keyboard so I can text message my buddies?" "I want mine smaller than anyone else, and I'll pay $1,000 for it." "I want mine to cook, clean, and detail my car." "I want mine to run my errands."

There are so many things we don't need on a phone, and to think we hardly even use it to talk anymore. Our phones have become James Bond gadgets that we can show off. My phone is already outdated, and I bought it in the summer of 2010. I remember in the late '80s, when people really didn't want to carry their cell phones around because they were a little bigger than a newborn baby. They were huge. Now there are little ear devices that make you look like you're taking someone's order.

Weren't these gadgets supposed to be for emergencies only? Now we can't do anything without them, and we deem them a "necessity." Everyone has one: kids, teens, dogs. These gadgets will quickly take over our personal lives if we don't band together and stop them. We must take a stand. When you are with your wife and kids, turn it off. Undivided attention doesn't mean text messaging your buddy you saw at work an hour ago. At least during dinner, give your wife and kids some time without them hearing the latest rap song come out of your cell phone as a ring tone.

It's all about her idea #103: Take walks at night around the block

Do this not because you had a fight and she wants you out of the house to cool off. Do it because you know she's a mom and she'll appreciate it more than you know. This walk accomplishes several things. It's a few minutes of alone time away from the kids. It gets you out of the house together, and you get a bit of exercise. If it's cold, don't go too far. If it's too hot, go later at night. Be forewarned, your wife will likely point out what she likes about the neighboring houses that she would like you to do to yours—like plant a Japanese rock garden in the exact shape of the yin-yang symbol.

It's all about her idea #104: Comfort her when she cries

It's probably your fault anyway. A hug, a rub of the hand, a kiss on the cheek, or a soft word make all the difference to a woman when she's hurting. Many times, all a woman needs is someone to listen—without offering a "quick-fix remedy" or an opinion. Women are stronger than men, we know that, so it doesn't take much to comfort a woman who is hurting. It doesn't matter why she needs comfort, but who else is she going to get it from? She can call her mom or best friend, but she likely needs more than that. She needs the one person she's closer to than anyone else—you. (Besides, do you want a thousand questions from your mother-in-law on her next visit about where you were when her daughter needed you?)

It's all about her idea #105: Let her choose the restaurant

It's not like In-N-Out Burger is not exciting for the one hundredth time in three months, but she needs to choose a restaurant for once. Hamburgers and fries are considered a romantic dinner in some parts of the world, but her taste might vary. Most women have an eye for good cuisine, whether American or other, so let her pick out where to dine once or twice, or always. You may have to put on dress slacks, but I'm sure the food will be good.

Chapter Ten

After You're Done, Do More

*"That married couples can live together day after day is a
miracle the Vatican has overlooked."*

—Bill Cosby, author, actor, and comedian

We've all seen those guys before; we've even huddled
around the water cooler and talked about them for
hours. You know who they are. They're the men who do anything and everything just to please their wives. They're the ones
who write *good* books about romancing your wife, not the ones
who are filled with sarcasm and cynicism.

Every woman loves (or at least appreciates) this type of man
because they go the distance in their relationships. They get things
done on time whenever they need to be done. They never have
an excuse. They never complain. They overextend themselves and
even write poetry. They're full of surprises. They make their wives
laugh, not cry. They can change a diaper and talk interior design
at the same time. They're cordial. They're smart. They can cry at a
chick flick, and most incredibly, they don't have one feminine bone
in their bodies. They can relate to women so well because they're
perfect on the inside, not necessarily on the outside. They're sensitive. They're aware of their women's feelings, and they're tuned in.

What's up with that? They must be whipped or something. I bet their wives wear the pants in the house. Do they not have a backbone? They actually care more about hanging out with their family than with us at the gym or at a pizza place? Are they trying to make the rest of us look bad? If they are, they're doing a great job. How many men have had that conversation before? A lot. Want to know how you can become that guy?

Up until now, every chapter has focused on husbands being a part of their wives' lives by giving more to a marriage than just money and sex. Those things are great, but in the end, they fade quickly, and women want something more fulfilling. They want a guy who is kind and sensitive as well as manly and responsible. A great husband and a great father. The guy husbands hate and never want to be. The guy that all women love to have around the house as their love slave. The guy who doesn't care about being called *whipped* by his friends. If you want to be the dream guy whom you're talking about, you can be. The guy that can do no wrong in the eyes of all females because he's one hundred percent dedicated to making his wife and kids happy. Some men stop short of being this guy because they don't want other men thinking that they're not a "manly man." Evidently, that's the staple of manhood: being known as a "guy's guy."

I remember a time when my wife and I took dinner to a couple who had just had a baby. When we got to the house, my wife went straight to the kitchen and started to prepare everything for the couple. That meant setting the table, getting the silverware out, ice in the glasses, napkins and bowls, everything.

I was on my way out with the father when my wife turned to me and said, "Honey, I need your help." As I began to walk toward her, without hesitation, my friend said, "Dude, they got it. Let's go outside. I want to show you my new toy." Of course, *toy* in manly lingo can mean anything. It could be a new car, truck, lawnmower, four-wheeler, boat, video game machine, or any contraption with an engine or loud noise. I then said, "It's cool. I can come look after I help her set up." He then snickered and said, "Okay. Whatever." So we both went back into the kitchen and helped get dinner ready, or at least tried to.

My wife and I didn't know where anything was, so we kept asking the mother of the newborn. The reason we were asking her and not the father was because he didn't know where anything was. The mother was sitting down at the table instructing all of us, including her husband. I'll be the first to admit that I don't know where a lot of the stuff is in my house, but this guy didn't know anything. Not because he just forgot, but because at that point, he had never helped his wife in the kitchen—with anything, at all, ever…in his life.

For goodness sake, he didn't even know where the ice cream scooper was. Stuff like that is important for survival. What about can and bottle openers? What about trash bags for when the pizza boxes pile up after the big game?

My wife's the one who puts everything up in our house, and I'm usually the one who gets it down. But I have eaten dinner by myself before and actually know where the dishes and silverware are. I also know where we keep the dishwashing soap, the toaster, and the salt and pepper. I help my wife with

Christmas and setting up for parties. I help her make certain dishes for Thanksgiving and even dress up for Halloween. This father didn't know his way around his own kitchen, much less the house. In hindsight, I'm not even sure if he knew who we were. Okay, he did know that, but they did have a lot of visitors over the span of two weeks. I'm sure everyone started looking the same after a while.

Learn the ins and outs of your house. Know where everything is, not just the remote and batteries. God forbid, your wife may be sick one day and need you to take control of her position as foreman of the house. What are you going to do, call your mother or mother-in-law? What if they live in another state? What if they can't get there? What if they just laugh hysterically at you over the phone? What if you're in a town where no one knows you? What if she's sick with the kids? Are you prepared to do everything and anything within your power to make sure everything doesn't fall apart? Are you ready to face the unthinkable? Are you ready to give up all control of your manly activities and put them on hold to care for your wife? Are you willing to change your normal manly routine and give of yourself? That may mean doing things like holding her hair back when she's throwing up, feeding a six-month-old in his highchair as his head bobbles back and forth, setting all the appointments, scheduling all the activities, and even doing things like cooking dinner. Combine that with the rest of your wife's list and then pile it on top of what you do currently.

That's what this chapter is all about. You'll be that guy we all make fun of. You will just need to stop having conversations with those other guys because now you'll be one of the "whipped" ones (and yes, I am speaking from experience). Pretty soon, we'll all be reading the book you write.

It's all about her idea #106: Make it easy for her to have a ladies' night

Plain and simple, if she wants to have a night with the girls, don't just *let* her do it, but *help* her do it. Actually, "let her" sounds extremely chauvinistic. You're not her master. You should never have to "let her" do anything. Agreeing with her about going out with the ladies sounds a lot better. There's nothing wrong with a little time away from you. There's nothing wrong with a lot of time away from you. You both know she spends plenty of time working at home or working at an office, or both; whichever it is, she deserves a night out with the girls. If she does go out, don't ever keep score. That will certainly put a damper on the whole thing. Don't remind her that she's gone out more than you have. While you're at it, your wife should never have to ask, "Can I go out?" She's not sixteen, and you're not her daddy. My wife and I like to use questions like, "Do you mind if I go out with the girls?" and "What do you think about me going out with the guys?" That way, you're getting her opinion, or she's getting yours.

It's all about her idea #107: Hug

It's that simple. It's not sexy. You don't have to throw each other on the bed and slobber all over each other. You just stand there and put your arms around each other and squeeze. Do it for thirty seconds, a minute, or half a day. You can even go a little beyond the hug and grab something. You may catch her off guard but also surprise her. (Of course, if you're in the doghouse, this surprise could lead to a slap.) This little thing may be just the needed relief to get her through a stressed-out day. Try a hug before work and right when you walk in the door. And since you'll be getting good at hugging, don't forget at least one a day for each kid.

It's all about her idea #108: Buy a cookbook and make a special meal

Very Martha Stewart-sounding, but look at all of the shows your wife watches with male cooks and chefs. Maybe you're just as good as those chefs and you cooked when your wife was pregnant due to the nausea stage. Either that, or you spent all of your time at the fast food joints. Either way, you're not doing it for you now; you're doing it for her. Sure, you didn't take home economics when you were in high school. I don't know anyone who did and brags about doing it. That's okay. I didn't take home economics either, but I know how to read instructions and make something like oven-roasted tomatoes with goat cheese and sautéed scallops. This may take some time away from *SportsCenter*, so be prepared to go all the way with this. Whether it turns out to be a fiasco in flames or perfection on a plate, she'll be impressed it wasn't another night of mac and cheese.

It's all about her idea #109: Don't golf for a day or two or three or four

I am a scratch golfer. Which means every time I golf, I end up scratching my head, wondering, "What am I doing here?" I hate golf. This is on the list because once men get hooked on this sport, it can quickly become their number one priority. Golf lessons, balls, the right equipment, course and cart fees, driving to the course, golf outfits, and shoes all contribute to less time and money for the family. Ministers, athletes, college students, doctors, disk jockeys, actors, and musicians are some of the people who play and spend plenty of time bragging about how good they are. I like the sport and don't mind telling people I'm actually a scratch golfer. It's a recreational delight, but hanging out with your kids or doing yard work should rank higher on the list

It's all about her idea #110: Renew your wedding vows

With a fifty-one percent divorce rate in the United States, maybe we should do this every weekend, just to remind ourselves what we actually said in our vows. There's no official rule that says you have to have this done on a certain anniversary year. I know some people like to do it on the tenth, fifteenth, twentieth, twenty-fifth, or fiftieth wedding anniversary, but I'm sure any minister or justice of the peace could do it on the third, fifth, seventh, and eleventh anniversaries. It doesn't really matter—just have it done. It's exactly what it says it is: going back over the vows you took years ago and refreshing your memory on all the promises you said you would keep. This time around, it'll be a lot more special because maybe your kids can be there. Plus, you can have the ceremony somewhere different, instead of a church or courthouse or the den of your mom and dad's house. Maybe next time it can be at a beach on a tropical island, a mountaintop overlooking a gorgeous valley in Ireland, on top of a skyscraper, or at a private party with a group of close friends on a yacht.

It's all about her idea #111: Take a bath or shower together

Yes, that's exactly what I'm saying. I want you to get buck naked with your wife, get in a hot bath or shower, rub lotion all over her body, and do something you probably haven't done in a while: *relax*!!! Relaxation should be your main focus. Don't think about the kids, daily stressors, the boss, bills—think about absolutely nothing but your wife. This may not be comfortable for you. You're right. It's not comfortable cramming your six-foot-four-inch frame into a small tub while stewing in tepid water. On top of that, she throws in the candles and bubbles, and you feel down-right feminine. You think your wife cares about that stuff? No way. She's just thrilled you're with her. Actually, she's just thrilled you can fit in the bathtub without all the water going over the top.

It's all about her idea #112: Spa day

Only if #111 doesn't really do it for her. You change your car oil every three thousand miles, right? This is her oil change every three thousand miles. A massage, a new 'do, a pedicure, a manicure, a facial, aromatherapy, any of these is ambrosia to her soul. It's sort of a retooling for your wife. Women love spa days because they are one hundred percent relaxation time. No phones, kids, computers, cars, husbands, nagging moms, errands, calendars, or TV. It's just an hour or two with Hans, the good-looking masseuse with magic hands from Switzerland. If you don't have a spa where you live, agree to watch the kids while she's taking a warm bath and doing her finger- and toe-nails. Remember, if it's something that makes her feel better and you help to arrange it, she'll likely act better toward you.

It's all about her idea #113: Don't buy her clothes, but get her a gift certificate for her favorite clothing store

Ever hear these words from your wife: "This outfit doesn't fit me anymore. What happened?" The answer is, she had a baby. Don't tell her that though. It's a rhetorical question she really doesn't want answered. If you do respond, make sure it's positive and upbeat. It probably won't matter, though, because she's not looking for you to appease her with a pompous quip like, "You look fine. I can't tell a difference between before the birth and now." She's actually looking for a quick solution: either losing the weight or hiding the weight gain with new clothes. Since camouflaging is easier than losing the weight, you'll be prepared for that moment with a gift certificate.

It's all about her idea #114: Get the "snip-snip" (if it's still relative)

Sorry, guys, this doesn't mean getting a haircut, but does involve getting *something* cut. If you just quivered, you guessed it—it means getting a vasectomy. Whatever you want to call it—severing the big sperm tubes or pipes, a mini waterslide, or surgical sterilization—just get it done. Obviously, if you don't believe in this, don't do it. This is for men who are done having babies, and don't want their wives to have a tubal ligation. Not having any more kids is a pretty big decision to make, and understandably, this procedure would be hard to reverse. But it isn't a big deal. It takes just thirty minutes, and you'll be in and out of the hospital within hours. Recovery usually takes about forty-eight hours. Doctors will tell you not to do any strenuous activity during that time. That gives you an excuse to watch TV.

It's the least you can do for everything your wife has gone through. She may have already spent plenty of time in the hospital having kids. Don't make her go back into the hospital to get a tubal ligation. That's basically the female version of the "snip-snip." She has had a baby. Don't make it her responsibility to provide birth control for the family as well. Pick up some birth control, don't have sex, or get the big cut. If you don't do any of these, you're going to have a hard time convincing her the "natural family planning method" is going to work every time, especially if the "natural family planning method" is why you have kids now.

To add to that, if you're down and out for a few days because of the plumbing problem, make sure she is shown the appropriate affection. Men tend to forget that right after they've had surgery, but they always want women to hop into bed just days after delivering a baby.

It's all about her idea #115: Encourage her

Your wife has opinions, goals, plans, and ideas, so why not get behind her and support anything and everything she wants to do (as long as it's legal)? Whether it's being a mother of five, going back to school to get an education, working, traveling, writing, whatever, don't ever keep her future endeavors boxed in or on the shelf. Show her that you're not the only one who wants to succeed.

It's all about her idea #116: Know what quality time is and have it

Reading together in bed, a weekend alone, a walk, or a getaway to a bed and breakfast will build a relationship and is desperately needed if you have kids. This time is spent to have the in-depth conversations you can't have at the dinner table. To some, "quality time" means concentrated, uninterrupted moments to spend with children, spouses, or friends. It's believed that this time should make up in quality for what is missed in quantity. It should be relaxed and free of conflict.

It's all about her idea #117: Make Mother's Day a lot more special than any other day

This is one of the most important dates on the list. This day defines what your wife does or has done as the mother and giver of life to your children. Mothers look forward to this day almost more than any other in the year, because it's the day that high-lights their accomplishments as the keeper of your children. This is not your day! Plan something nice. I'm sure dinner and some flowers are fine, but think creatively. I try to always do something that will make my wife cry. If she sheds tears, I know she knows it was heartfelt. One year, I gave her a gift, and she didn't cry afterward. I figured something was wrong, so I went and got some onions and made her cut them up, so I could say she cried on Mother's Day. Anyway, get together with the kids and make it a joint effort. Do a trip to Paris, France, or even Paris, Texas. Just make it a day she'll remember.

It's all about her idea #118: Buy her a nice piece of jewelry

And it doesn't have to be expensive. In fact, grocery stores have jewelry for twenty-five cents up front in these little machines. Women love nice things, but there are two items they certainly love to show off—jewelry and furniture. Okay, three: their kids. All right, four certainties: their grandchildren. Okay, five: their hair. Okay, so the list never ends, but jewelry and furniture are things that usually last a long time and convey sentimental value.

That's why it doesn't matter if it's a big piece, a little piece, a necklace, a love seat, a bed, earrings, an ankle bracelet, a divan, or even an armoire. Women love to talk about their jewelry and furniture with other women. This doesn't necessarily have to be done as soon as you meet your wife. This can be done sometime in a lifetime, and no, you don't have to go out and pawn stuff off or sell your blood or marrow for this. You just have to listen to her and know what she likes.

It's all about her idea #119: Do something with your wife you may have done when you first started dating

Well, no not that, but you should be doing that all the time anyway, right? Actually, this is something different. Take her to a festival, go see a late movie and actually hold hands with her, make out in your car at a local park, look into her eyes—all are allowed with this one. Women like to take those long walks down memory lane, especially if it's about something you did when you first met. Pull out an old photo and have it blown up (not with dynamite, but at a photo place).

It's all about her idea #120: Plan a special day for your anniversary

The problem is most men plan it around their needs, not their wives' needs. Sure, Mixed Martial Arts events are fun and exciting, but maybe your wife doesn't want to be at an event where she can see a woman breast-feeding her baby while drinking a beer with the other hand (the mother, not the baby). Women have a top-five event list every year. Your anniversary is one of those. In fact, some call this the Super Bowl for women. To them, it's bigger than the NBA Finals. In their eyes, it's more historical than the Stanley Cup Playoffs. To the Major League Baseball title game, it holds no comparison. Next to their having babies and getting a new house, your anniversary stands to be a top-five event of their lives. That's where you come in. You have the power in your hands to make her the happiest person on the planet. You also have the power to make her the unhappiest person on the planet. It's an easy choice if you're smart. I can't tell you what to do or where and when to do it (of course, there are one hundred fifty great ideas for in the pages of this book to help you get started). If you are desperate for ideas, talk to her closest friends.

Chapter Eleven

Father or Friend?

"It is a wise father that knows his own child."

—William Shakespeare

Do you ever wonder what you'll say when you're sitting on your death bed and all of your family is sitting around you, watching and waiting to hear you speak those last words of inspiration before you kick the bucket? Will it be a joke? Will you tell certain people they're not in the will? Will you sing a song? Will you blurt out a bunch of drivel and saliva and make no sense at all? Probably. Most importantly, will you tell your children you should have spent more time with them instead of being at the office working eighty hours a week?

That's certainly something to think about now, because you won't have the time for anything but regret if you wait too long. You'll be a frail ninety-five-year-old geriatric at that point, and putting your loved ones on your knee to bounce around will just seem sad and pathetic. The same thing goes with throwing them up in the air or grabbing hold of their arms and spinning them around like an airplane. It'll all be gone. Why? Because you always had that one last deadline, or one last meeting, or one last deal to make, or one last trip to go on. So why not change that now and quit using those excuses?

If you ask men, they can tell you about certain types of bonding, the most popular being the kind that ties or adheres things to the wall. Other types include chemical bonding, commercial bonding, cap bonding for teeth, and bonding with a person to impact a relationship. That last one is what this chapter concentrates on. It's the bonding that most men have the most trouble with, and they actually participate in the other types of bonding just to get out of personal bonding. Way too many husbands lack something in their relationship with their wives because they don't put an emphasis on their relationship with their kids and the bonding they need. If you look at why that is, you'll come up with several reasons.

The "I'm busy" excuse is the world's greatest cop-out and most used among fathers. It doesn't make sense to a lot of people because having kids isn't a very good reason to ignore them once they're born. There are plenty of deadbeat fathers out there for that job. Your wife knows you're probably not that guy yet, so don't ever sink into that pattern of neglect. If you're already in that pattern, then this is the perfect time to change.

No one's quite sure when the "I'm too busy" excuse came into the picture, but no doubt it's still relative in today's world. And the thing about it is there's not really a good excuse for giving the excuse of "I'm just way too busy for my kids." Either you spend time with them or you don't. Saying you'll spend time with them and not doing it is just as bad as not doing it. They're both very detrimental to your kids. If your wife and kids know that you're not going to show up for that ball game or the dance recital, at least you didn't lie to them. Constantly saying you're going to show for something and then not doing so is way worse than not making the commitment in the first place. I believe the penalty for that should be sitting on the couch with your family and watching six hundred hours straight of *The Cosby Show*, *Little House on the Prairie*, *Leave It to Beaver*, *The Waltons*, *Growing Pains*, *Family Ties*, *Happy Days*, *Good Times*, *The Duggars*, *Jon and Kate Plus Eight*, *Little People, Big World*, *Moving Day*, *Sister Wives*, and *American Chopper*. Okay, forget *American Chopper*, I just threw that one in to see if you were paying attention. Basically, any and every show on The Learning Channel, because your wife and kids are hoping you actually learn something. Maybe that way you'll understand what it means to be a father that treasures family values more than the almighty dollar or plans with "the guys."

Of course, we all know those shows were made from Hollywood scripts by writers and directors, but some of them actually represent family values and give a great portrayal of how fatherhood should be in the "not so real" world of family. Each show goes through "real life" problems like teen pregnancy, drug use, relationship issues, and the loss of loved ones. The difference is, you live in the real world, so you can write your own script, and have the ability to meet the demands at work and balance the home life all at the same time.

My dad worked his tail off for thirty-three years at the same job and always made an effort to be at the beginning of a game or at the end of cheerleading tryouts, or at least he was home in time for dinner. He was always there for Thanksgiving and

Christmas and Easter Sunday at church. He worked hard and long and never complained about doing it, and he never, despite working four jobs at one time, never, ever, ever gave the excuse, "I'm too busy." I give him an A for the effort, because he forced himself to make the time, no matter how tired he was, and as a result, he really doesn't have a rear end anymore. Seriously, there's nothing back there. He has a flat bottom. You can literally play racquetball on it—it's that's flat. That's okay, though, because every time I see him, his flat behind reminds me that he was a great father, because he tried to be there for everything and anything my siblings and I, ever did.

My wife's father was the same way. If he had a business trip out of town during the week or a hunting trip ten states away, he would always be back by the weekend to spend time with her. Even Dr. Cliff Huxtable of *The Cosby Show* found time out of his busy schedule of being a gynecologist to spend time with Theo, Vanessa, Rudy, Denise, and Sandra. He had time because he shared the responsibility with Claire, his wife, the attorney.

Your wife is not a father figure. Don't force her to be that person. There's no way she can pull off swinging the kids around or putting them on her shoulders or getting down on all fours and playing horsey. You're supposed to do that. When your teenage daughter comes home from school with a friend, who is going to be there to make fun of them and ask them about the boys at school and joke with them about their goofy-looking clothes? You're supposed to do that kind of stuff, not your wife. She's busy enough. She's relying on you, her partner, to help out with all the cool, funny, crazy stuff.

If your relationship with her is different now than before the kids were born, that's okay. I believe that's why you're reading this book. Every couple goes through a transitional stage after the kids are born. Sometimes it takes days to get over it. Sometimes it takes years to get over it. If you're still getting over it, that's fine. But don't make your kids suffer for it. Don't make it look like your wife is the father and the mother, or like her father and your father play the role of daddy because you're not around. You have your own day out of the year set up just for you. It's called Father's Day. Be worthy of that title and spend time with your kids.

Be the guy that does everything. This list will certainly give you a head start on changing the way you do things. It will not only help you with your relationship with your wife but also with your kids. If your kids are young or old, they may not recognize that you're doing this other stuff for your wife. They may not realize that when you do these things with them, whether they're small or large, you're basically melting your wife's heart over and over again. You're not only enriching the lives of your children, but you're contributing to their future success while providing a good example of a great relationship. Turn off the Palm Pilot, let the secretary do it, file it for another day, call it in, get to work earlier so you can leave earlier, rearrange your calendar, or quit the job and get one that's more adaptable for your family. Just remember, that computer or briefcase may not fit in your casket when you're dead one day; memories will. They don't take up any extra space in your casket or in heaven. So why not make creating special moments a priority here on earth? (On a side note, I'm not sure about hell, though. I believe they allow one carry-on per father.) Whatever you do, force yourself to spend time with the most important people in the world: your family. Once you do this for a while, you won't have to force it. You'll see the rewards it brings to everyone you care about, and you will choose to do it—no forcing necessary.

It's all about her idea #121: Be involved with your children's activities

Shouldn't this be a given? Kids love nothing more than to be with their number one man. Of course, if you're not around, their number one man may end up being grandpa, by default. These activities would include athletic, dance recitals, school plays, camp, field trips, and church carnivals. Be the father who's up in front with the coolest video camera getting every second of your child playing the tomato in the school play, making the final shot at the buzzer, or pitching a tent. Letting them know you love them is one thing, but showing them how much you love them by attending events is way more important.

It's all about her idea #122: Feed the kid(s)

Breakfast, lunch, or dinner, shoving food in their little mouths doesn't take too much time, but it can be one of the most challenging things to do. Feeding a six-month-old mashed peas is like trying to refuel a car while it's moving. Your wife needs help in the morning getting the kids off to school, so taking five minutes to pour a bowl of cereal, butter some bread, scramble some eggs, or pour some juice shouldn't be a big deal. It will help all parties start off on the right foot. You don't want to go to work knowing your kids didn't get fed and your wife was disappointed in you.

It's all about her idea #123: Take a picture of the kid(s) and put it in a frame

I know men aren't supposed to do crafts, but this is an easy one. Take a picture of you and the kids or just the kids. Women love photos, especially framed ones. Go to your local Hallmark store or gift shop and choose a frame to your liking. Put the two together and surprise her with this gift either on the counter in the kitchen or the sink in the bathroom. She'll show it off to the whole world and proudly tell them you did it "just because."

It's all about her idea #124: While dining with the entire family, take the kids to the restroom

Trust me, your wife gets to make the daily trek to the bathroom and engage in "wipe duty" more times than the average basketball team scores in a game. Now that you have taken the family out, keep the positive momentum going and take over bathroom duty. Let her relax and sit in one spot for more than six minutes—a rarity she will appreciate. If your kids are all grown up with kids of their own, be the cool grandpa and impress your kin by taking the grandkids to the restroom.

It's all about her idea #125: Let her sleep while you rock the baby

Get up; grab some Joe; check out all of the real estate, knives, getting in shape, jewelry, and food infomercials on the tube; and start pacing or rocking or patting or singing. I actually read some of my old college books to our second child. They usually put me to sleep in class, so I was trying to see if they worked on her. Let your wife refuel for the big day ahead. You can always sleep at work during your meeting with the boss.

It's all about her idea #126: Read the instructions for your kids' toys

Unless you're McGyver—able to make a walkie-talkie out of a toothpick, orange peel, and safety pin—this one's especially for you. So when it comes to fixing or putting your kid's toys together, take time to read the instructions. Whether it's a play-set or remote control car, safety is the main issue here. You don't want something breaking down and causing bodily harm.

It's all about her idea #127: Give the kid(s) a bath

It's not a water park, but pretty close to it. This is the next best thing to a water park. Kids love it because they get to splash Dad, soak in the bubbles, and play with the toys. (I've heard that studies show this is one of the best ways to bond with young ones.) You will love this, since you get to splash, be obnoxious, clean your kid, and play with some cool water toys. Kids love warm baths, especially before they go to bed. This is quality time that shouldn't be rushed. If you have knee trouble, grab some towels and put them underneath for comfort, or pull out a pair of kneepads from your soccer days. You can also try a small stool that you can sit on next to the tub.

It's all about her idea #128: Help with the kids' homework

I'll be the first to admit that I wasn't an A student in junior high or high school, so this one is pretty tough. I was actually a pretty good student until I had to take algebra—something that I am convinced was invented in hell. I can barely spell, much less add. I was the type of kid who, when the teacher approached me with a graded exam, she would turn it over and fold it in half when she gave it to me. She would also clear her throat and give me the raised-left-eyebrow, crooked-mouth, look of disgust. That meant only one thing—a bad grade. Usually, I hoped and prayed for at least a C, because then I knew that I could still play sports. I would grab the exam, turn it over, see a 73 percent, and shout out, "Do you believe in miracles?"

Of course, the A students that sat around me were doing the same thing, but they were hoping and praying for an A with bonus points. If the teacher offered five bonus points on a test, and they got just three bonus points, they were usually the type who would literally cry. You know those types of people. You see them all the time. They're called doctors and engineers.

I, on the other hand, was celebrating the fact that I didn't fail. I eventually went to college with that same type of thinking. When I graduated with a GPA of 1.95 and they rounded it off to a 2.0, I did what those A students did back in junior high; I cried.

Sure, you don't know squat about calculus, world history, or biology, but you know how to use an object lesson with apples to add and subtract. That's what your kids want (unless they are in high school or college—then they might laugh at you, but that's okay, too). They don't want a stuffy, old, all-about-the-numbers math teacher at home. They want their cool and funny dad to explain algebra on a practical level, even if he has to use his fingers and toes. Our parents didn't know too much about science and geography, but we turned out okay. Didn't we?

It's all about her idea #129: Snuggle with the kids

Definitely fun to do in cold weather, but it can be done anywhere and anytime. Put in a movie, fix some popcorn, make some hot chocolate, and make a memory. This can be done in bed with Mommy or in the family room with everyone. From birth, kids love to be close to their parents. We have two perfectly good, expensive leather sofas in our home, but my daughters always want to snuggle on the hardwood floor. They also want to make a fort or hiding place with the cushions from the leather sofas. Cuddling with your wife could also be an option when the kids aren't around to do the snuggling. You can either do it in bed, on a sofa, on the ground, in the car, in the movies, in the shower, camping, or just standing up. You can do it in warm weather, in cold weather, in the desert, at the beach, on a plane, or on a train. Remember those wedding vows and the line "to have and to hold"?

It's all about her idea #130: Discipline the children with love, not anger

If your kids have ever said, "Quit yelling at me," and you responded with, "I'M NOT YELLING!" you need to read this. Yelling and screaming has never worked on kids, so if you do it, I would suggest you stop. You only make yourself look like an idiot who is unable to reason, while frightening and confusing your children—and maybe your wife, too. Eventually, they might start emulating you and yell at your wife, other kids, the dog, and their stuffed animals.

Many times, I find myself telling my oldest daughter to stop yelling loudly to get her little sister's attention, but then I do the exact same thing when I'm instructing her. Child experts say this is not the correct way to discipline a child, and I certainly agree. But I also know that my three-year-old has the lung capacity and volume of most grizzly bears and large elephants. My wife and I believe she inherited them from a great uncle on my side, who was a drill sergeant in the Army. Also, when your kids are in school and having a fight (or the thousandth fight) with another student, you will feel like a moron when sitting in the principal's office because your child was yelling inappropriately. It will be hard to tell your child not to yell when he is looking at the principal and saying, "That is how my dad does it."

It's all about her idea #131: Have family night

That means everyone, not just your wife and the kids hanging out at Chuck E. Cheese, a mall, or a carnival. You complete the unit. Get the work done and leave it at work. You're the hero to your kids, the knight in shining armor to your wife. Get in the SUV and take a field trip to the local bowling alley and go nuts. Eat food you haven't eaten in a while. Be goofy. Throw a gutter ball just to get a reaction from the little ones. Put the kids on your shoulders, throw them up and down, dance with them, dance with Mommy, throw Mommy up and down. This is your time to clown around and not worry about what anyone thinks.

It's all about her idea #132: Take the family camping

Most kids today have no idea what camping is. For that matter, most men don't know what camping is either. Their kids live in the world of the "concrete jungle." That would include skyscrapers, malls, theaters, schools, and amusement parks, not to mention what's on the inside of schools, malls, theaters, amusement parks, and even their homes. You now have digital TV with five hundred fifty channels, video games, movies, and computers.

The digital world has taken over their little brains. That's where you come in. This is a great way to show off your "macho" skills and live off the land while getting away from the daily diversions of life and having true quality time. Pack up the SUV, grab the sleeping bags, get the cooler and all of the supplies, and hit the nearest lake and recreation park. It doesn't matter if you're Smokey the Bear or Ranger Rick, your kids will love the idea. And if they don't, wait until they catch their first fish, start their first fire, share their first ghost stories over marshmallows, pitch their first tent, see a deer for the first time, or make their first s'more. They'll be like that first fish—hooked for life.

It's all about her idea #133: Read to your children

How cool is that feeling knowing that when you do this, your kids will be getting valuable tutelage from their main man? It's not from a teacher, a tutor, a learning video, or even Mommy. The stories you read them will last forever. This can be done anytime, but kids love it when they're about to hit the sack. Try voices, characters, noises, and even weird sounds. Of course, if you're reading them a Tom Clancy book, the voices and noises may not be necessary, but if it's *Timmy the Tonka Truck Goes to Town*, then they're perfect. If you are incredibly bored by children's literature, read a chapter book you find interesting, one chapter at a time, with you being the amusing narrator.

It's all about her idea #134: Work as a team with rules of the house

If you've ever played the game kids like to call "Daddy is a gullible idiot, so let's ask him instead of Mom," you understand what I'm talking about when I say work as a team with your wife. You know how this works. Kid goes to Mommy and asks her if it's okay to play outside. Mommy says no, and Kid then goes to Daddy in the other room. Kid bats the baby blues and asks Daddy if it's okay to play outside, and Daddy says yes, not knowing Mommy already said no. Mommy looks for Kid later, but doesn't know where she is. Mommy then asks Daddy where she is, and Daddy says she's outside. Mommy tells Daddy to get a brain and realize he just got played by a four-year-old and then goes outside to get Kid.

Kids are smart when it comes to playing their parents. Work together to put a stop to it. It's not always obvious to us because women are usually around the kids a lot more than we are. When your wife says no, consult with her when the kid comes batting those baby blues.

It's all about her idea #135: Go to the PTA meeting with your wife

Either that or the parent teacher conference, whatever it's called these days. Show up and act like you're interested in your child's welfare. What do you think *PTA* stands for? *Pay total attention* to what's going on. This is where you get to find out if your kid is developing into the next Einstein or he's on his way toward a lucrative future of summer school. This is also where your wife gets to show off "Dad of the Year." You're the coolest dad on the block, but no one at school knows it because you never show up to these things. Either that, or maybe you're not the coolest guy on the block, because you don't go. If you ask most men, they couldn't tell you what their kids made on their last report card or what their teacher's name is from year to year. Don't be part of that group. Be the guy who bugs the teacher about every detail of your kids' class. My mother was a teacher for twenty-five years; they love it when dads get involved.

Chapter Twelve

Do You Still Like Me?
Yes ( ) No ( ) Check One

*"An archaeologist is the best husband any woman can have:
the older she gets, the more interested he is in her."*

—Agatha Christie, author

Monotony and redundancy are a huge part of marriage. It happens to every couple, young or old, after one year or fifty years. Every day, couples can get caught up in the same routine over and over again, and repeat the same process every year. It's not anyone's fault. It just happens, especially after kids are on the scene.

From a man's perspective, it is get up, go to work, and come home. From a woman's perspective, it's get up (if there are kids, this could be really early), go to work, come home, do housework, feed and get the kids to bed, do some more cleaning, try to find time to eat, and then go to bed moments before it is time to get up again. If your wife works at home, it's just about the same schedule, with kids, triple the stress.

That's why many couples try to keep their relationship fresh, unique, different, and rejuvenated. How do they do that? Anything that gets you away from the same old rut would probably work. These are extra things that add some spunk and spice to a dull marriage. Spontaneity helps, but maybe you're not that type of person. That's okay; you can fix that. You just need to get rid of all your inhibitions and be prepared for a different reaction from your wife. Remember, at this point, she thinks you're as exciting as morning breath. Sure, you're good at your job, you get along with others, you're a good son, and you love your kids and wife. In today's world, that would be enough for us, but by today's standards, your wife needs that "extra stuff."

The mystery is trying to figure out what that "extra stuff" is and how it'll help you go from ho-hum to hot. Don't try too hard, though, because you don't want to go from boring to deranged. You do want to go just far enough for her to see that you are changing.

There are couples who never venture out and try any other types of food besides steak and potatoes. Every Friday and Saturday night, it's the same old, dull, under-cooked, medium rare steak down at the grill house. Don't get me wrong—I love steak. But what about sushi, Indian, Caribbean, Lebanese, and Italian? Or how about picking up a guide to local restaurants and just trying something new? My wife and I like to go "outside the box" and explore new tastes. If we don't like them, we move on and try something different. Does there have to be that much adventure when you eat? No, but it does give us a good chance to talk about what new restaurants we'll be going to, the ambience we like, and the types of new desserts we get to indulge in. Planning a vacation could be the same.

The extra stuff doesn't even have to be that extra. It could be small gifts. When my wife worked away from home, I would put her birthday or anniversary cards in the seat of her car or under the visor or on the dashboard, someplace where she would not notice them until she got to work. I used to stick them in her purse, but they actually got lost among the 113 items already in there. Since she became a mother and works full time at home, I had to find a new place to put the cards. I chose a place I knew she would frequent several times a day to take the kids—the toilet. It's not the most romantic place on earth, but while she was potty training our two-year-old, it was probably the most visited. I would either prop them up on the seat (it was closed, of course) or on the top part where a picture or towel would go. She thought it was romantic and was glad she had reading material while she waited three hours for our child to go potty.

To go along with the card thing, my wife likes a certain candy that no one else on this planet dreams of buying, much less eating. They're called Circus Peanuts. Yes, they are an actual candy item, not the salty, round things. They're orange, marshmallowy, and sugary peanut-shaped pieces of goo. They look like the packing foam in boxes. To me, they taste just like the packing foam in boxes. To her, each one is a small piece of heaven. That's really the only candy she ever eats, so I know when I get them for her, she is appreciative. It takes her away from the hustle and bustle of her day. You can't get them just anywhere. You have to either special order them or try a dollar store outlet. Of course, I know Circus Peanuts don't do the trick when it comes to adding that extra punch of zest to our relationship, but it's something different. It's going beyond myself and thinking of something I can do for her. It doesn't matter what it is, your wife will appreciate it.

If you take a look at most couples, they usually do in their relationship what they do to their expired food in the refrigerator.

They throw it out. They discard it. If it smells stale and old and has mold growing on it, they get rid of it. If it looks like a science project in the making or is dried out, no matter what the cost, they chuck it in the trash. There's nothing worse than drinking a nice cold glass of cola that has no fizz. What about pouring clabbered milk into a big bowl of hardened Cheerios? It's downright gross. You obviously don't want your relationship to be like clabbered milk, because you're reading this book. If your kisses and hugs and nightly outings have no sizzle and your conversation has no fizz, maybe it is time to add some unique sparks.

This final list will get you started. Short of taking her to the tropical island of Fiji, these simple ideas will not just make you look like Mr. Surprise but will also show your wife you care enough about your marriage to do different things every once in a while.

It's all about her idea #136: Go to that marriage seminar

Paying money to hear other men say, "You're a horrible husband," sounds fun doesn't it? Do it after the one-, three-, or seven-year itch or even the thirtieth year. Why? Not to sound like a facial cleanser ad, but to rejuvenate your marriage and observe other couples going through the life experiences you are. This is the time when you realize that there are other couples that have the same dysfunction you guys have. These aren't only for people who have problems. They are a place to receive information on how to prevent problems. You'll find a seventy-year-old couple who have been married for fifty years and next to them will be newlyweds married just a month. This isn't the place to sit and say, "See there; I was right, and you were wrong." If you're lacking something, like intimacy, this may be the place you find it, if you want to.

It's all about her idea #137: Take a day trip just to get away from it all

Away from what? For you, it's work, sports, your car, bills, and other stuff that doesn't really matter. For your wife, the list is a lot longer: kids, work, the house, day-care, school, lunches, carpool, PTA, meetings, doctor visits, scheduling, soccer practice, and dance class. My wife and I once visited a city three hours away from where we lived just to go eat at a restaurant that served the best Mexican food in the state. Of course, once we ate, we had to stay the night because we were both in full bloatation mode and we couldn't move, much less drive back. We stayed the night in a hotel and made our way back home the next day, very slowly. The trip probably cost us about $100 overall. It was spur of the moment. We didn't plan it or think about doing it. I just swept my Cinderella off her feet and put her in the coach and we took off.

It's all about her idea #138: Make breakfast, maybe even in bed

Do it on a day when you can have plenty of time to cook and prepare a great meal. Don't wake up late one morning and decide, "This is the day," and go wake her up to give her a breakfast bar and banana. Make it worth her while. Do it on a Sunday. It's supposed to be a day of rest, so let her stay in bed and even recruit the kids for help. If they're gone, do it yourself. You're not Chef Emeril Lagasse and that's okay. Your wife understands. He has nine restaurants in his name, two TV shows, and eight cookbooks that have sold more than two million copies. All you need is to microwave some bacon, heat up some waffles in the toaster, scramble some eggs, pour some juice, cut up fruit, and get a tray to put it on, and guess what? You'll end up starting your day with a happy wife.

It's all about her idea #139: Send her flowers

A very good idea, but worn out. Flowers are God's creations and are certainly appreciated by women from all over the world, but they are used on too many occasions such as having a new baby, weddings, funerals, birthdays, saying congratulations, Valentine's Day, and get well wishes. If you're going to send these, make it on a day she's not expecting it. Do it while she's at work or working at home. Write a special note to go along with it. If you do it all the time, it may turn into a big waste of money, and the idea may get old as fast as the flowers do.

It's all about her idea #140: Make a video

Video cameras cost next to nothing these days. Most families have access to one and put them to good use. How come you're not doing it? Is it because you don't know how to, or because your eight-year-old son knows how to work it better than you? Whatever the stall tactic, get over it and start filming. Women love to sit down with a big box of tissue and be entertained by family videos, especially if there are children in them. With editing stores all over the place, you'll be able to get help with background music, computer imaging, picture enhancement, whatever you need. If it sounds like a lot of work, it is. Remember, she birthed a watermelon for you. Just file that little nugget of information somewhere in the back of your brain so you can think about it every time you talk yourself out of doing something nice and memorable for your wife.

It's all about her idea #141: Request a song on the radio

Very cheesy and very '80s, but very, very funny. She's sure to get a kick out of it or end up kicking you for doing it. Young or old, it happens all the time. "I'd like to request a song for my wife, Judy. Could you please play 'If You Won't Leave Me, I'll Find Someone Who Will'?" Rock, country, soul, or jazz, without a doubt it'll send her into an adolescent frenzy, thinking she's back in junior high.

It's all about her idea #142: Paint a picture

Sometimes you don't necessarily need to buy her the same flowers over and over and send them like it's a new idea. It's sweet, but they die within days. The same goes with perfume. She smells great already. Why not spend that money on something she'll appreciate a lot more? Who cares if you painted outside the lines when you were little? Go to your local craft store, pick up a canvas (small or large), buy some paint and a few brushes, and create something unique. It could be a photo of her, the kids, fruit, the *Mona Lisa*, dogs playing poker, or a self-portrait. If it turns out to look like a five-year-old painted it, even better. Have you seen what people have in their homes hanging on the wall? Some of that stuff goes for tens of thousands of dollars. All you did was spend a few bucks to make your wife smile. She can hang it on the wall or hang it in the garage; whichever it is, no doubt she'll brag to her friends about having her own personal Picasso.

It's all about her idea #143: Have a picnic

Yes, it's not a seaside beach or even a park underneath the Eiffel Tower in Paris, but it is romantic and something you can easily do. Grab some sandwiches, chips, fruit, and dessert, and go outside, in the backyard of your house, to the park across the street, or to a hilltop overlooking the city. It doesn't matter. She'll love it and think the idea is very *Love Story*.

It's all about her idea #144: Be considerate of her temperature needs

Unless you're a bat and sleep in a cold, dark cave at night, you really need to consider doing this. This basically means when she's cold and you're hot or vice versa, you should be willing to negotiate a compromise. Most women have a smaller body mass index than their men, so they are likely to be colder more often than their brawny husbands. If your wife is anything like mine, the thermostat can read 78 degrees and she'll say, "Honey, I'm freezing. Turn the air off." She will be wearing layers and I will be sweating, as I lay bare-chested and barefoot in boxers on the bed. When we roll over to spoon under the covers, her backside often feels like a frozen rump roast straight out of the deep freeze. It's hard to believe that a human being who is alive and has a pulse can be that cold to the touch. She often seeks to warm her ice cube–like toes on my calves by using a surprise attack at bedtime. It's almost as shocking as jumping into a swimming pool in Chicago during November. We have also had some pretty major "discussions" about thermostat control while en route to an event or a date. They usually start with, "I'm hot," or "I'm cold." Just take my advice: Give up the control, stick your head out the window like a dog, and your life will be much better.

It's all about her idea #145: Throw her a surprise birthday party

I know this is a tough one because men aren't good at keeping secrets and forming plans about something this big. We either screw it up by recruiting the wrong people or accidentally telling the wrong person. The first rule of success is, don't be a chatty Patty and tell the whole world. Recruit some help, but not much. The more people who know, the faster it gets out.

The best location is at her favorite restaurant in a private room. Just make sure she doesn't recognize any of the cars when you guys pull up. She thinks you guys are getting a cozy table in the back room and voilà! *Surprise!* People she likes, and some she may not, jump out and scream and holler. Just knowing you planned it all by yourself without too much help from her friends or family should bring either a smile to her face or tears to her eyes.

It's all about her idea #146: Write her a note

This is different from a card. A card already has a message in it from an unknown author or someone your wife doesn't know. That could be used as a cop-out for writing something meaningful. A note can be used to write down what might be hard to say face to face. It doesn't have to be worded perfectly. It doesn't have to rhyme. It doesn't even have to make sense. This should come from your heart, not from another card.

Don't ever buy a card that someone has already written and then copy the message on to your blank card. Women can tell when you've done that. If you were in college and you tried that on an essay, it would be called plagiarism. You would get a big fat zero on your paper. It doesn't have to be funny, smart, or witty. It can be totally stupid, dumb, lame, and moronic. Just do it, and see what kind of result you get.

It's all about her idea #147: Find her a good piece of furniture

Just like jewelry, women love to show off their homes and what's in them. You may be the king of the castle, but it's also her castle, and she wants to fill it with good furniture. Not the stuff you used back in your college days that smells like dirty feet and sweat, but stuff that looks and feels good. People don't know this, but there are furniture outlet stores with discount prices all over the place. You can find one by going online or searching the local papers and outlet directories. Ask designers or check out antique stores. Even ask those whose homes you admire.

It's all about her idea #148: Share a candlelit dinner together

Women want to be swept off their feet. A sports bar showing the title game doesn't do it for them on a night away from the kids. Take her somewhere nice and quiet. Candles may get her in the mood for something else—like dessert. If she doesn't go for the quiet dinner, find a quiet place like a library or funeral home.

It's all about her idea #149: Purchase a quirky gift

A blender, vacuum, toaster, waffle iron, a newspaper mention, a radio shout out, or a dinner cruise—she's sure to be surprised on a different level and maybe even annoyed at first. Before she gives you that weird look or wonders why you spent money on it, explain to her that it's supposed to be quirky. It's also supposed to be something she didn't necessarily want or use, but something she'll definitely tell everyone she received.

One Christmas, I gave my wife a blender. I told her it was the kind she pointed out to me when we were walking through a cooking specialty store. This wasn't any ordinary blender. This had high-speed everything. It had dual controls, six-speed manual transmission, exhaust pipes, ergonomic speed controls, and a supercharged thirty-two-valve, high-flow intake and exhaust. It was fuel injected with a rear spoiler, ground effects, low-profile buttons, capacity canisters, and could make fifty smoothies in thirty minutes. This thing was the mac-daddy of all blenders. Of course, that's what I thought. She gave me a "Why would you waste money on a hideous device that's going to quickly make its way to the garage sale item rack in the basement?" look.

That's exactly what I wanted, because hidden inside the top of the blender cover was a jewelry box with some very hot ice in it. She eventually found it and exploded with relief and joy, all at the same time, and surprisingly changed her thoughts about the blender.

It's all about her idea #150: Give her a deep, slow, long, wet kiss

Kiss her the way you did when you first met. Everyone remembers those kisses. Weren't they delicious? The question is, why don't we still do it? Maybe because we're older, and we're not filled with lust anymore. Maybe halitosis has taken over, and it's considered gross now. I mean, they still do it on soap operas, and they make it look like it's still fun. Have we forgotten how to do it? Maybe it just seems weird. Maybe we're all in such a big hurry these days, and pecks on the lips and cheeks are all we have time for. Maybe we got creeped out when we saw Vice President Al Gore kiss his wife the way he did at the 2000 Democratic convention. It was sort of a forced, smashed, off-center, jaw breaking, "I'm going to hurt you with my lips" type of kiss. Maybe your wife doesn't do it anymore because you're disgusting.

The point of the whole thing is to start off slow. Don't mess it up by cramming your slithery tongue down her throat. She doesn't want to gag every time. She's not kissing Gene Simmons. She's kissing the man that helped her bring children into the world, the same man that sleeps with her, showers with her, plays with her, and eats with her. Let her enjoy it the way she did when you guys were dating.

• • •

Congratulations! You took the first step in becoming a better husband and father. You read *150 Secrets to a Happy Wife*. What now? Well, put into practice what you read. Maybe you already perform most of the ideas on this list. If you do, maybe it's time for you to write a book, and tell us how you're doing it and continuing to do it every day for the rest of your wife's life. If you're not using these ideas and never want to, well, I'll leave that discussion to you and your wife. So you better get with it and start making your wife a happy person. But before you start, there's just one more list of things that you need to read that's sort of a reminder about what we say to our wives.

Chapter Thirteen

Things to Say to Your Wife If You Want to Die Immediately

Dumb: lacking intelligence or good judgment; stupid

—www.dictionary.com

It is only fitting to end this book in the same manner we began—highlighting dumb things men say. If you ask most men what the dumbest thing they've ever said to their wives was, they would probably hesitate and say something ridiculous like, "I don't really recall anything I've ever said that's dumb." And the reason why they hesitate is because they're probably trying to remember the dumbest thing out of many dumb statements.

Ask their wives the same question, and they can't answer fast enough. Not only do they remember the statement, but they also know the dates, time, where you were, the context in which it was used, how offensive you were on a scale of one to ten (ten being the worst), what you were wearing, whether she cried or not, whether you cried because she hit you after you made the dumb statement—they remember everything.

Asking newlyweds this question is fun, because it seems as if they're real careful that first year of marriage. They try to steer clear of dumb statements, so the response is something like, "We really haven't said anything dumb to each other. We're just so in love." Asking people who have been married for a long while, that's a different story.

I posed the question to my wife's grandparents (who have been married for more than fifty years), and they came up with a couple of doozies. Of course, just like every other couple, there was some debate on who told the correct version and who tried to weasel out of the story as if they didn't remember. For the purpose of being factually correct, I submitted her grandmother's version, as her grandfather's was somewhat cloudy.

Her grandmother told me that one particular time, before they got married, they were on a date, taking a midnight stroll alongside an open field. They lived in Oklahoma, so there were plenty of fields, and that was considered a date. She wanted to look her best for the man that would someday be her husband and the father of her kids. Looking her best meant even her nails had to be all dolled up. This particular night, she covered her nails with a lovely shade of candy apple red. They didn't have nail salons back then, so if you wanted long nails, you had to actually grow them. That's exactly what she did, and that's exactly what she thought her man would appreciate—long, pretty, red nails.

Suffice it to say, he didn't. In fact, he said one of the dumbest things he could have ever said. While he was holding her hand, he looked down at her nails and said, "You know that when we get married, those things have to go?" Now before I finish the story, let me interject the fact that it was still a trial-basis relationship. The jury was still out on whether they would have another date, but with comments like that, the jury probably wouldn't have come back in. So with the dry wit my wife's grandmother possessed, some consternation, and a raised left eyebrow, she replied, "We may not get married." Now, for some reason, after that, his boldness waned just a bit until they got married, and years later, he would find himself in the same predicament when he was trying to be funny.

My wife's grandparents lived on a farm where they worked all day in the fields with horses they liked to call Scrubs. They weren't thoroughbreds or racehorses of any kind. In fact, he would tell you that they were the opposite. That's why when the horse would do something that was out of character for a "Scrub," folks would say stuff like, "Not bad-looking for a Scrub."

Well, he decided to try the phrase out on his wife, who was pregnant at the time. One morning, as they were preparing to go to work, his wife came out of the bedroom with a new dress on. She did a few spins, waiting for him to get the full image in his mind and shoot back a compliment, but instead he said, "You know, you don't look half bad for a Scrub." Details are a little sketchy about what happened afterward, but by God's grace, he did survive the comments. Years later, he would blame the insensitive moment on the fact that he had a lack of blood and oxygen to the brain that early in the morning.

I know that we, as men, could probably compile a list of hundreds of thousands of things we should never say to our wives, especially during an argument. However, it seems that the list below consists of some of the most popular things that have been said and continue to be said. Omitting them from your vocabulary could very well lengthen your life.

1) "Are you going to wear that?"

Not only will you see the tears flow from your wife, but you may actually get something thrown at you (maybe this book). You likely aren't a fashion icon—you can barely dress yourself. You think Adam walked around the Garden of Eden telling Eve, "I can't believe you wore those fig leaves today. Why not wear the azaleas tomorrow?" It wouldn't have happened.

Your wife has had kids. Next to them, her body is the most important thing in her life. It's the machine that runs your household. It's the thing she's trying to always keep in shape for you. So when you question what's hanging on it, you're basically telling her that what she's wearing is not good enough. Sure, she may not be able to fit into those tight jeans she wore before she had kids. That's fine. You may think it's an innocent question, but it's not.

Now if she is wearing an outfit that's made of chain link only, by all means question away. However, if it's not showing too much skin and she's comfortable in it, I would just go ahead and leave it alone. If she asks you how she looks, don't say, "Good." She'll end up saying something like, "Just good?" Say she looks great, and don't make a weird face when you say it either.

2) "What did you do with your hair?"

First of all, it's probably none of your business what she does to her hair. If she wants to put a dead cat on top of her head, she can do it and shouldn't get any flack from you. Obviously, that would be very gross and very weird, but the point is, she shouldn't be questioned about what she does to her hair—it's her hair. So she pays another man $50 to "make her look beautiful," who cares? She's happy with the strawberry blond highlights she got instead of the mocha brown highlights she asked for, so you should be, too.

3) "What is this we're having for dinner?"

Just like I tell my kids, "Eat it, or you'll go to bed hungry." Of course, I never really stand by that, but they end up eating what is placed in front of them anyway and go to bed happy. This is the goal for you—ending up in bed happy and with a full stomach. That can't happen, though, unless you eat what your wife cooks. If it's different than what you usually eat, add something to it. My wife is a great cook, but every once in a while she'll cook a piece of meat, fish, chicken, or pork that's bland. And by bland, I mean it's been cooked, but just not dressed up with anything else. On the very rare occasion when that happens (hey—she's going to read this), I go to the spice rack, refrigerator, or pantry to see if there's anything I can use to put on it (salsa, hot sauce, steak sauce, salt, pepper). Oh, and don't ever say, "This sure doesn't taste like my mother's." You may get a crock pot thrown at you—while it still has hot stuff in it.

4) "You're not pregnant, are you?"

She better be or you just called her overweight. When you go up to a woman in a grocery store and ask her when she's due and she says, "I'm not pregnant," that's bad enough, but saying it to your wife is even worse. This statement is actually an equal opportunity offender. When you say, "You're not pregnant, are you?" is that because you don't want her to be and you weren't expecting it?

A friend of mine was on a business trip when he got a call in his hotel room from his wife. After a few minutes of banter, she came out and said, "I'm late." Now, when women use this term, it means one of two things. If they're late for an appointment, they'll usually say, "I'm late. I have to go." All she said was, "I'm late." He knew immediately what that meant. But instead of saying something with intellect, he paused slightly and said, "You better get going." Needless to say, it was insensitive and not taken well by his wife. Just like his wife, women know that saying, "I'm late," or "I'm pregnant," can be overwhelming to men, especially if a baby wasn't in the picture or you thought your protection worked. So instead of jumping the gun on this one, let her come out and say it first. If she is pregnant, you don't want to start things off on the wrong foot when you say something dumb.

5) "You think your day was stressful? Let me tell you about mine."

Did you have to clean spit up off the carpet, hear screaming half the day from a six-month-old baby with colic, go pick up formula, clean the house, take the dog in for shots, have a mammogram, and fight a nervous breakdown? No, you didn't. Unless you did these things, or more, don't ever get caught playing the game,

"Who worked harder today, you or your wife?" I promise you, you will lose this game every time you try to play. This is how it would go: Contestant number one (that's you), at 8:00 a.m., you arrived at the Smith, Henson, and Jackson accounting firm. You parked your car, rode the elevator upstairs to the fifth floor, and walked into your office. Your secretary, Donna, brought you your coffee and schedule for the day. She exited your office, and you immediately went online to find out what the scores were from last night's football games. About 8:15 a.m., you began working on the same audits you were working on from the day before. At 10:30 a.m., you took a potty break and stretched your legs. On your way back to your office, you saw Mike from payroll and chatted a bit about the upcoming weekend. You got bored, so you headed back to your office. Before hitting the audits again, you checked your online stocks. You wrapped up the morning by getting an early lunch at 11:40 a.m. You were back in the office by 12:40 p.m. and continued work on the same audits. That took you to 3:00 p.m., where you met with the office manager and several other accountants in the boardroom. That went almost until 4:00 p.m. You went back to your office and called your friend Ted to set up a tee time on Thursday. You put the wraps on the audits and headed out the door around 5:10 p.m. You were in the elevator by 5:13 p.m. and out of the garage by 5:16 p.m., So what's so hard about that? Congratulations, I think you have the easiest job in the workforce.

Now let's take a look at contestant number two. Your wife woke up at 4:00 a.m. with the baby, who wouldn't stop crying and likely has an ear infection.

You awoke a couple hours later complaining that your back hurt because you slept funny. You wondered why you got no empathy from her as she was contorted into an odd shape in a rocker with a screaming baby. In the other hand she had the phone because she was trying to see if someone could cover for her morning presentation while she ran Junior to the doctor. Of course, none of her coworkers were answering or were likely dealing with their own equally stressful morning.

She took the baby to the doctor then swung across town to the pharmacy where she got stuck behind an elderly man who was filling all eighty-seven of his prescriptions. Frantically, she finally got the prescription and ran Junior across town to her mother's who reminded your wife that she should have given Junior those special earmuffs she knitted from wool from the wild beasts her father killed and then maybe he wouldn't have gotten an ear infection in the first place.

Forty-five minutes later, she drove back across town to arrive at work a little before lunch. Her childless boss gave her a condescending once-over as she entered just as the presentation concluded.

When she sat down at her desk, the phone rang. It was her mother. She was questioning the prescription she was supposed to give Junior because she had never heard of the antibiotic and it didn't come up on her WebMD.com search (which she performed on the computer you thought was a good idea to get her for Christmas). Fifteen minutes later, she was off the phone and canceled the lunch date she had made so she can catch up on the forty-five messages that piled up in her absence. Her stomach was hungry, but she couldn't eat because she was too worried about Junior. Her boss called her in that afternoon and said that her colleague Jim had been able to save the day on the presentation. It was no coincidence that Jim happens to be the one colleague she doesn't see eye-to-eye with. She returned to her desk, worked a little later than normal to try and catch up, and then raced across town to pick up Junior, who still has a fever but is sleeping.

Her mother informed her she was fifteen minutes later than she had promised. Your wife headed home realizing she never thought about dinner despite her hunger. She stopped at the grocery store and grabbed a few needed ingredients. She arrived home after 6:00 p.m. only to find you sitting in the Lazy Boy being a lazy boy, without thinking about starting dinner. "What's for dinner?" you asked when she entered. "I had a long day, and I'm famished," you added, licking your lips.

6) "You're acting just like [insert bad word]."

Some people think that if a man tells his wife she's acting like a certain type of bad word, she immediately gets offended. That's probably true, and most women would get upset if they heard that. However, I know plenty of women that would be more upset if the "bad word" were something other than an actual curse word.

I used to work with a lady whom I really didn't like. She tried so hard to make me mad all the time, and she did a great job of doing it. A lot of people can sympathize because they may have someone at their job that is just like her. I would go home at night and tell my wife about her. She eventually got accustomed to me talking about her. One day, instead of calling her by her real name, my wife nicknamed her Cruella De Vil, after the evil villain in cartoon movie *101 Dalmatians*, emphasis on the *De Vil* part.

I could tell that my wife really disliked this woman. So one day, while my wife and I were having an argument, I told her, "You're acting just like Cruella De Vil," but I used her real name. I could have said anything else after that, but she wouldn't have heard it. What I said had more of an effect than any curse word I could have called my wife. I know some men tell their wives they're acting just like the sister they don't particularly like or compare them to their mothers. Women don't want to hear that, either. Of course, men try to get out of this by saying, "I said you're *acting like* that, not that you *are* that." That logic won't work. Whether you think they're *acting like* something or you think they *are* something, they're still going to get offended. Just don't say either of them.

7) Maybe the dumbest thing you've said before is actually the thing you didn't say

You're probably wondering, "Huh?" Let me explain. When I prepared for this part of the book and asked my father if he remembered the dumbest thing he ever said to my mother, he told me he could remember plenty of things, but the time he didn't say anything was way worse than anything he could've said.

He explained to me that the company he worked for had sponsored a night at the local amusement park. That meant they rented the park out to make it a night of fun and excitement just for the company employees. After he and my mother got off a ride, they started walking toward the food court area. As they walked up to the food stand, two coworkers approached them. They waved and went over to greet my parents. When my father shook hands with the men, he turned and looked at my mother. This is the part that goes into slow motion. He called out their names and was preparing to call her name out when all of a sudden he said, "Guys, this is my wife, *blank*" (this is the part in radio we like to call dead air). He didn't say *blank*, because he didn't actually say anything. He drew a blank. He actually forgot her name!

After about five seconds of awkwardness, she blurted it out. My father tells me that it was one of the most embarrassing moments in his life. He said they just all kind of laughed uncomfortably and moved on with the rest of the night. As soon as they walked off, he says he couldn't stop apologizing. My mother just smiled and acted like nothing was wrong. Of course, all the while, she was probably thinking, "You blankety-blank!" Get the picture now?

8) "I HATE _____" (fill in the blank)

This could be one of many things. "You" is the most popular one among married couples, usually said during heated arguments. It could be "your perfume," "your cat," "your family," "your guts," "your bad breath," "the way you clean this house," or "the way you look at me with that condescending attitude."

All of these are used to express the way you feel about certain things that involve your wife and the world she lives in.

When you say the word *hate*, you're reaching in the deepest, darkest depths of your inner being and pulling out the most harmful artillery you can during a fight. Now, obviously, some people use the term jokingly, referring to something that's annoying but overlooked. If you're using the word to bring out a negative reaction from your wife during an argument, *hate* is definitely your word. It shouldn't be used, but is. Unfortunately, the echo of arguments in the bedroom spill over to the little ears that wander the halls at night looking for a glass of water. Your kids may hear you use this word and start using it themselves.

9) "Here's one more thing I can't stand about your mother."

There's no need to ever go here. Whatever you say, you're doomed, and for goodness sake, don't ever make a list, especially if it's negative. If you do, don't ever tell your wife about it—or your mother-in-law. If you're actually trying to say something nice, it will probably come out sounding cynical and demeaning, so don't even try. If you happen to get along with your mother-in-law,, mark it up as a success and count yourself lucky or blessed. Either that or you're doing a great job of acting like you like her. Mothers are wives' best friends times ten. Don't ever forget that. And don't ever forget that your mother is also a mother-in-law. You wouldn't want a list of negative things said about her, either. (Oh, and even if your wife complains about her own mother, don't make the mistake of joining in. Your wife has the PMS excuse to fall back on—you don't.)

10) "The baby's being way too loud. Please take him into the other room. I have to get some shut-eye for work."

Here's an idea: Instead of shut-eye for work, how about a black eye for work? That's probably what you're going to get if these words spill out of your mouth. Guys should not speak without thinking. It's called tact. If we ever say what we really want to say, would we still be married (or alive, for that matter)? No. Not only should you not say this, but don't ever use "the tone" with it, either. That tone is what women pick up on. It's that, "Hey, I need sleep way more than you do, so do you mind going somewhere else with our baby and making the noise in that other place besides here?" tone. It's called unsolicited sarcasm. It's when you're trying to be sarcastic, but you shouldn't. Telling your wife to go somewhere else isn't going to work. She should never leave her comfortable bed to take the baby anywhere. She probably chose the bed anyway, and here you are trying to kick her out of it. You should get up and go somewhere else. When it comes to sleep, your wife should get all of it. Don't ever complain about being tired. It won't pass, and saying the other nine things in this list probably won't either. Good luck!